WHAT TIME
IS IT?

ALSO BY A.G. SMITH

with Robert Livesay

Discovering Canada: The Vikings
Discovering Canada: The Fur Traders
Discovering Canada: New France

WHAT TIME IS IT?

A.G. SMITH

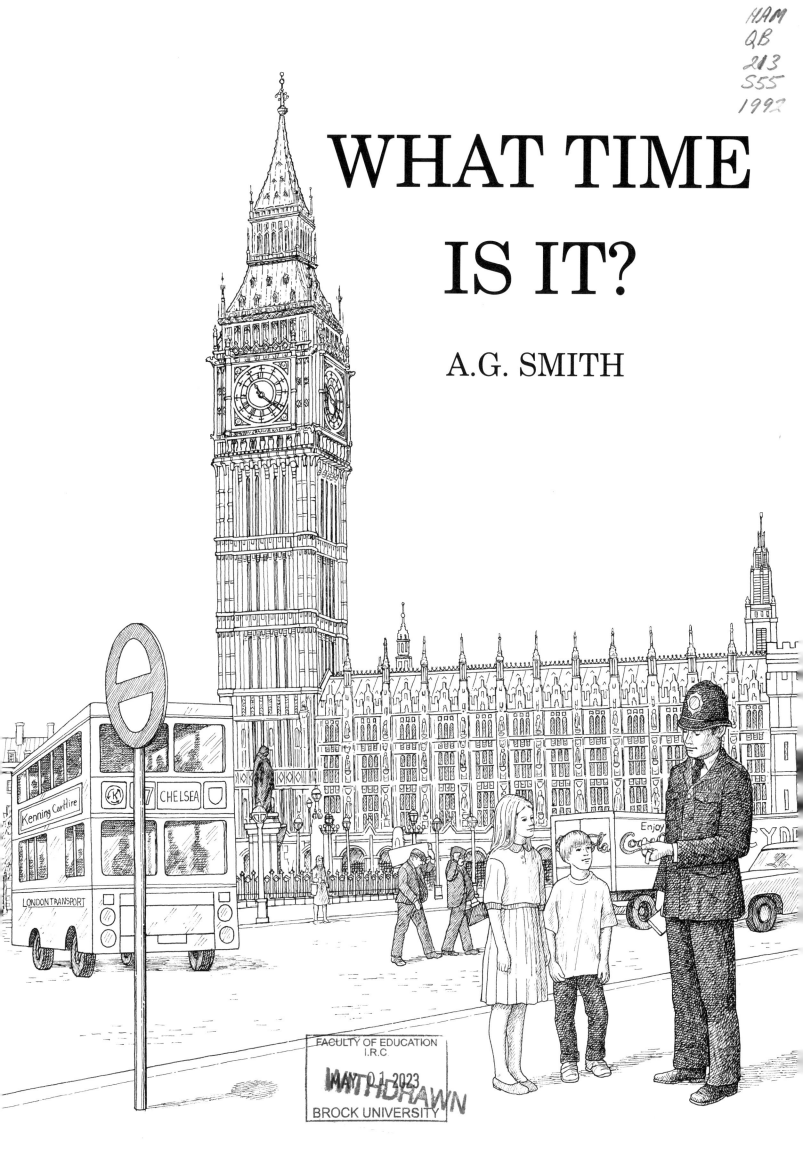

First published in 1992 by
Stoddart Publishing Co. Limited
34 Lesmill Road
Toronto, Canada
M3B 2T6

Canadian Cataloguing in Publication Data

Smith, A. G. (Albert Gray), 1945-
    What time is it?

ISBN 0-7737-5525-X

1. Time measurements — History. 2. Calendar — History.
3. Clocks and watches — History. I. Title.

QB213.S65 1992   529'.7   C92-093642-3

Cover design: ArtPlus Limited/Brant Cowie

Printed and bound in Canada

for my parents

CONTENTS

WHAT TIME IS IT?

From the very earliest days, human beings have based their time systems on changes in nature. People observed the sun rising and setting and saw the moon growing larger and then smaller. Some noticed birds disappearing in autumn and returning in spring. Since their success as hunters and farmers depended on their being able to predict the coming of the first frost or the return of certain animals, they soon learned to calculate the length of time between the changes.

Even today, people who live close to the land tell time by looking at nature. The Inuit, for example, know the seasons as the Time of the Seal, the Time of

the Goose, and the Time of the Caribou. During the long winter, they do not ask how many days have passed. Instead they say, "How many sleeps ago?" In the endless months of darkness, there is no "night" or "day."

Before clocks and watches were invented, people who based their activities on the changing seasons were thinking of time in a *chronological* way. That is, they saw time as a series of events, happening one after the other. Some ancient peoples, however, did not place much importance on this way of viewing time. More important to them was the way they felt events from the past and present blended together.

Today, the aborigines of Australia still think of time as a blend of past and present. Their lives are closely connected with the past through what they call "dream time," or eternal time. They believe that things are as they are today because of events that occurred in the deep past. In dream time, present and past flow into each other. Mythical beings such as the Eternal Emu live at the same time as 20th-century automobiles and steamships.

This ability to reach back into the eternal dream time of gods, heroes, and mythology gives meaning to the lives of the aborigines. Perhaps the desire of modern-day office workers to "get back to nature" on a two-week holiday shows their need to get away from chronological time and enter dream time.

Once holidays are over, however, most people living today view their lives as passing through chronological time. As societies have become more complex, time has been defined in more detailed ways. Days have been divided into hours, hours into minutes, minutes into seconds, and seconds into milliseconds and even nanoseconds.

Now our lives depend on doing things at particular times. We set our alarm clocks to wake ourselves up at a certain hour so we can get to school or work on time. We eat our meals at fixed times and we usually go to bed at about the same hour each night. Time has become an important part of our lives.

In the rest of this book we are going to find out where the concept of time came from and how it has changed over the years.

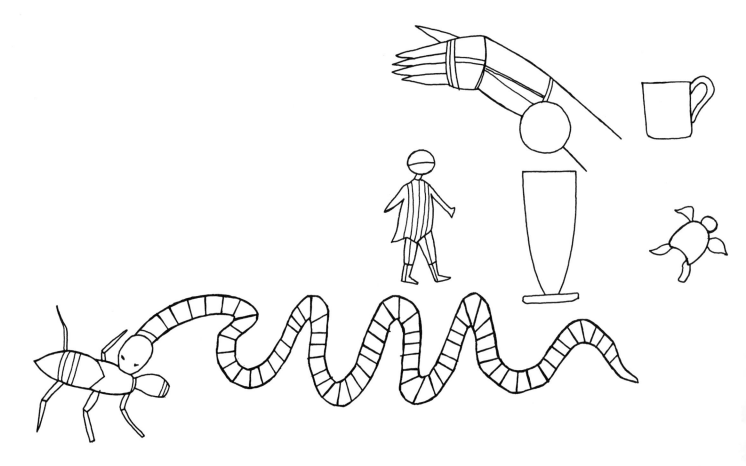

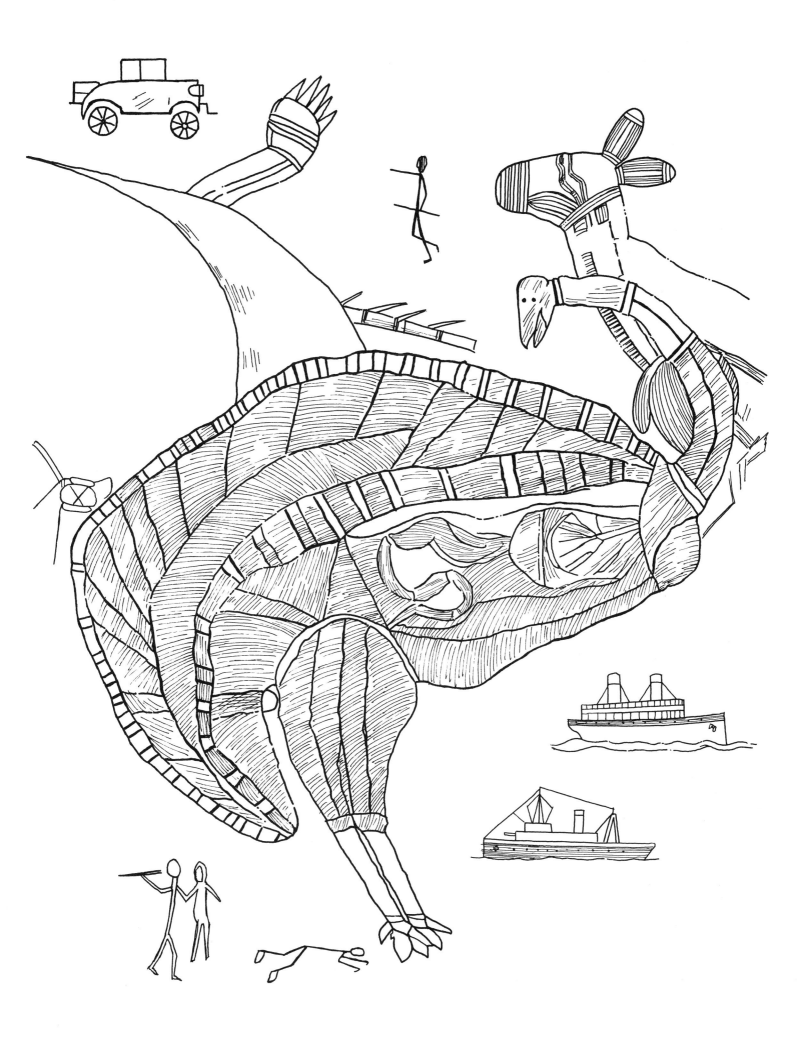

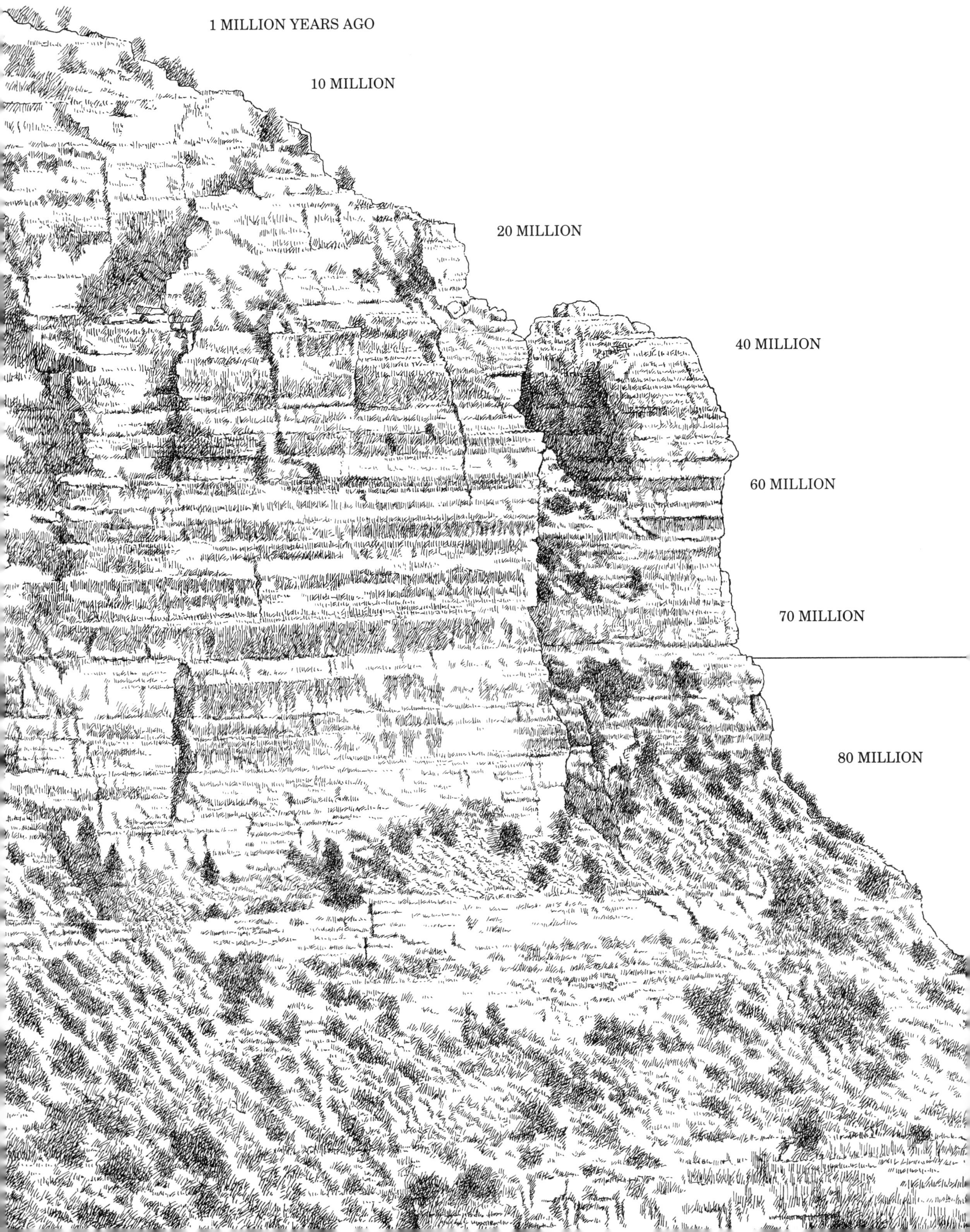

1 MILLION YEARS AGO

10 MILLION

20 MILLION

40 MILLION

60 MILLION

70 MILLION

80 MILLION

Curious scholars have always wondered about the age of the earth and the creatures that have lived on it. In 450 B.C., the Greek historian Herodotus found fossils of shellfish in the Libyan desert. This did not make sense, because shellfish cannot live on land. Herodotus concluded that the desert must once have been under the Mediterranean Sea. Since many of the fossils were of species that no longer existed, Herodotus asked himself another question: How long ago had these shellfish lived? Religious authorities later thought that fossils were records of plants and animals that had lived before the Flood. Some people believed that, according to the scriptures, the Creation took place on Sunday, October 23, 4004 B.C. Others did not accept this explanation.

In the 19th century, Europeans began to study the rock layers, or strata, that could be seen in the walls of gorges. They discovered that each layer contained different kinds of fossils. Their conclusion was that the different layers and their fossils were from different time periods. There were so many layers that they decided the earth must be much older than people had thought it was.

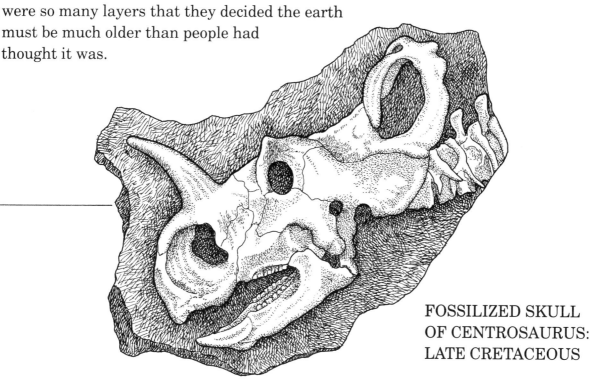

FOSSILIZED SKULL
OF CENTROSAURUS:
LATE CRETACEOUS

Fossils of tropical plants were also found in the Arctic, and glacial debris was discovered in Brazil. Findings like these showed that the earth had undergone great changes over long periods of time. In 1858, Charles Darwin published a book called *Origin of Species*, in which he suggested an explanation for these changes. According to his theories, the earth came into being many millions of years earlier than most people had thought.

The discovery of radioactivity in about 1900 provided geologists with more precise methods for dating the age of the earth. This is how geologists now use radioactivity to tell time: Radioactive elements such as uranium and radium

decay at fixed rates. In the end, they become lead. By measuring the amount of uranium in a radioactive rock against the amount of lead in it, geologists can determine how long ago the rock was formed. Scientists now believe the earth came into being between two and five billion years ago.

Radioactivity is also used to find out the age of plant and animal remains. All living organisms contain radioactive carbon 14, which decays at a fixed rate. By measuring the amount of decay, scientists can discover how long ago a plant or animal died.

TIME AND TREES

Trees are the largest of the plants on earth, and some of them live for centuries. The Bristlecone Pine and Giant Sequoias of California, for instance, are between four and five thousand years old.

Trees in temperate climates (north and south of the tropics) grow a new layer of wood each year. Scientists study the annual growth rings of trees that have been cut to determine their age and the conditions under which they grew. The close rings near the center of the tree show that when it was young the tree was shaded by others and received little sunlight. The variations in the later rings of the mature tree are marks of such variable conditions as years of more or less rainfall.

SECTION OF A 100-YEAR-OLD TREE

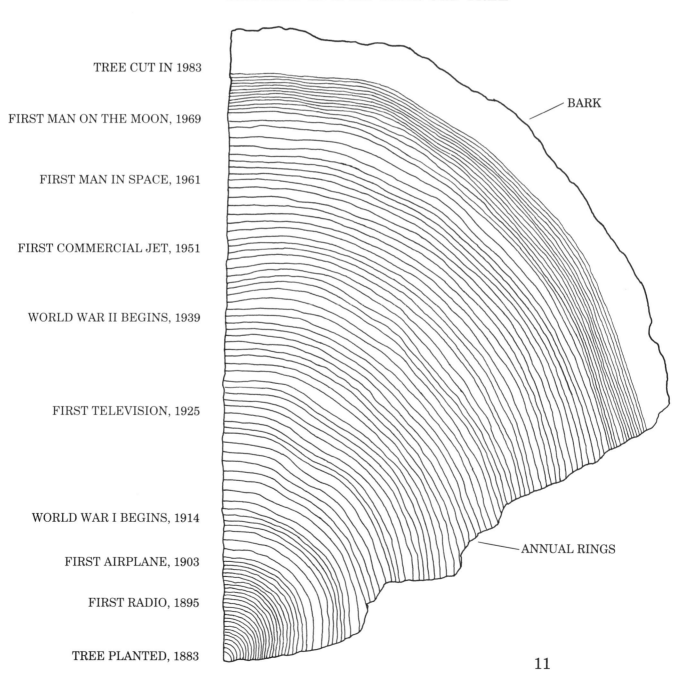

TREE CUT IN 1983

FIRST MAN ON THE MOON, 1969

BARK

FIRST MAN IN SPACE, 1961

FIRST COMMERCIAL JET, 1951

WORLD WAR II BEGINS, 1939

FIRST TELEVISION, 1925

WORLD WAR I BEGINS, 1914

FIRST AIRPLANE, 1903

ANNUAL RINGS

FIRST RADIO, 1895

TREE PLANTED, 1883

11

BIOLOGICAL CLOCKS

The activities of many plants and animals are controlled by internal "biological clocks." This is a short way of saying that their systems are set up so that they naturally do certain things at certain times. Some animals have bodies that tell them to sleep at night and stay awake during the day. Other animals sleep during the day and stay awake at night. The flowers of some plants close at night and open again in the morning. Biological clocks also affect the ripening of grain and periods of fertility in female animals.

Biological clocks may provide the answer to a question that humans have asked for centuries: "How do birds know when to start migrating?" Migration time would be easy to explain if birds left for warmer regions *after* the weather turned cold. But this is not what happens. They actually begin to migrate while the weather is still moderate and food is still plentiful. What guides young birds to their winter destinations a month after the adults have departed? Perhaps their biological systems are constructed in such a way that they migrate when their bodies "tell them" to.

THE SOLAR SYSTEM

Our solar system consists of the sun, its nine planets and the minor bodies such as comets, asteroids and meteoroids that circle around it.

Mercury is nearest to the sun, at a distance of 36 million miles (about 58 million kilometers); Pluto is farthest away, at 3 billion 666 million miles (about 5900 million kilometers). The inner planets, Mercury and Venus, orbit the

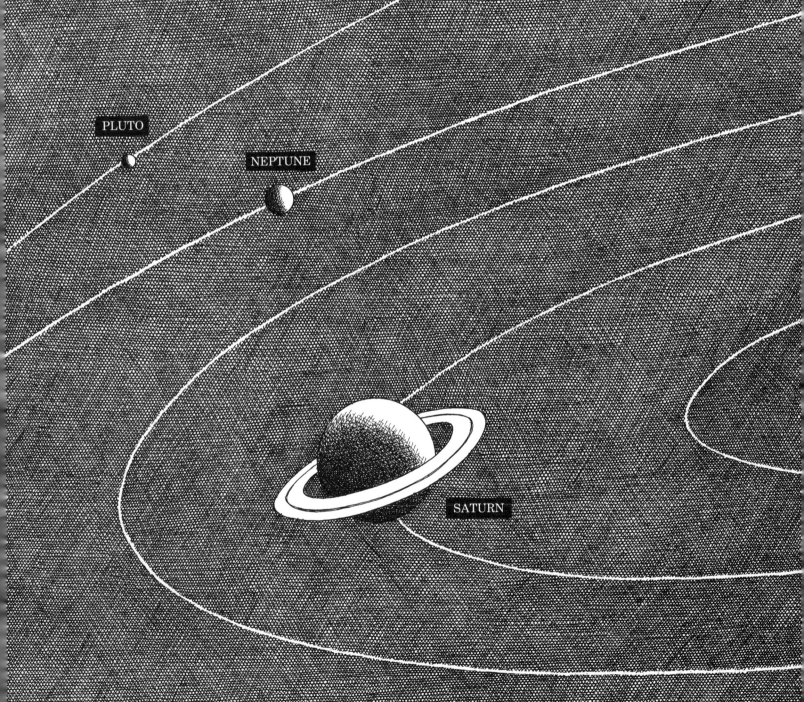

PLUTO

NEPTUNE

SATURN

sun in less time than the earth and therefore have a shorter *sidereal period*, or year. The "year" on Mercury is only 88 days long. The outer planets — Mars, Jupiter, Saturn, Uranus, Neptune and Pluto — have longer sidereal periods. It takes Pluto 247 ¾ earth years to circle the sun!

THE EARTH AND THE SUN

The planet on which we live is in constant motion. Although we do not notice this motion as we live our daily lives, we are actually travelling through space at approximately 68,000 miles per hour (about 100,000 kilometers per hour) as the earth makes its annual journey around the sun. This journey, or orbit, takes 365 ¼ days and determines the length of our year.

As the earth moves around the sun, it is also spinning around its own center, or axis, like a spinning top. If it did not do this, one side would always be facing the sun and the other side would always be in the dark. Instead, the earth does a full rotation on its axis every 24 hours, the length of our day. This gives all parts of the earth both darkness and daylight every 24 hours.

If the earth is like a top spinning around its axis, it is not an upright one. The gravitational pull of the moon and sun makes it slant in one direction. It is this slant, or tilt, of the axis that causes the seasons to change in temperate climates.

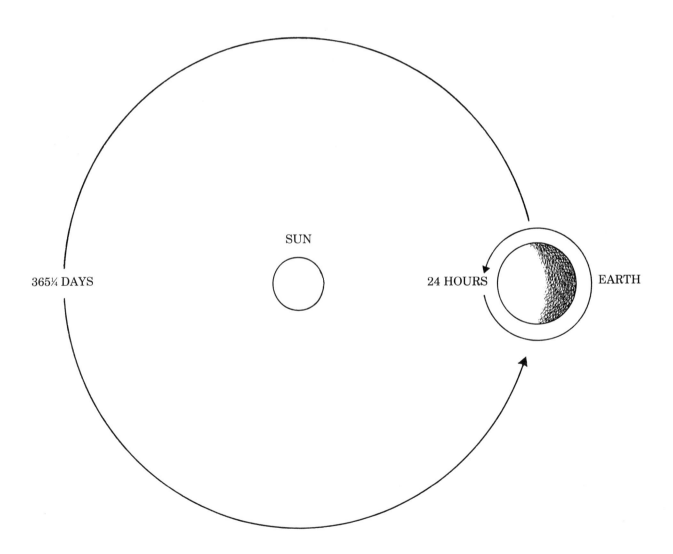

SUN

365¼ DAYS

24 HOURS

EARTH

THE SEASONS

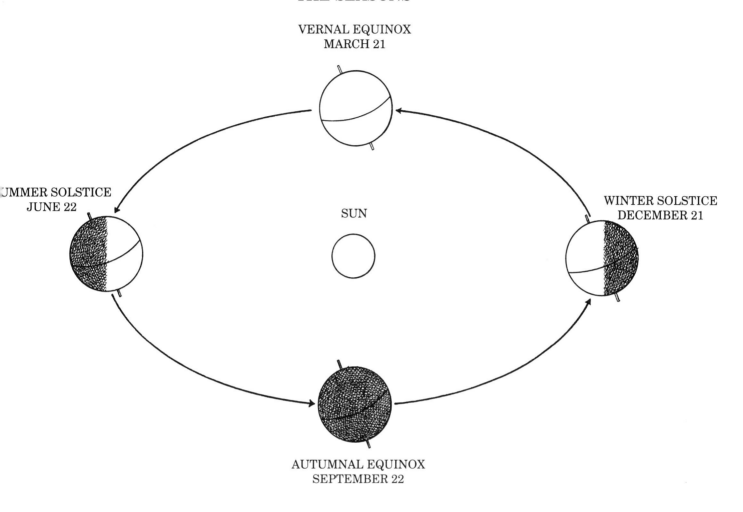

VERNAL EQUINOX
MARCH 21

SUMMER SOLSTICE
JUNE 22

SUN

WINTER SOLSTICE
DECEMBER 21

AUTUMNAL EQUINOX
SEPTEMBER 22

Because the sun strikes the regions near the equator equally all year, there is little or no change in climate in the tropics. It is hot in all seasons!

The illustration above shows the earth in four different positions in its yearly orbit. In the position on the far left, the top of the axis (the north) is slanted *away* from the sun. This means that the sun's rays hit the northern half of the earth (the northern hemisphere) less directly, causing cooler weather and shorter days. This is the northern winter. In the position on the far right, the top of the axis is slanted *towards* the sun, which means that the sun's rays hit the northern hemisphere more directly, bringing warmer weather and longer days. This is the northern summer.

The shortest day of the year in the northern hemisphere occurs on about December 22. That day, known as the *winter solstice*, is when the earth slants the farthest away from the sun (23½ degrees). The longest day of the year occurs when the earth's axis tilts 23½ degrees towards the sun — on about June 22. That is the northern hemisphere's *summer solstice*. Halfway between the summer and winter solstices, on about September 22, the *autumnal equinox* takes place. On about March 21, the *vernal equinox* occurs, signaling the first day of spring.

THE EARTH AND THE MOON

Just as the earth orbits around the sun, the moon orbits around the earth. It takes the moon 27 days, 7 hours, 43 minutes and 12 seconds to make one orbit — a bit less than a month. This is called the moon's *sidereal period.*

Since the moon makes only one rotation on its axis each time it revolves around the earth, it always keeps the same face toward us. Half of the moon is always illuminated by the sun but the portion that we can see varies as the moon revolves around the earth. These changes are called *phases of the moon.*

Imagine yourself standing on the earth as shown in the illustration on the next page. If you looked into the sky at night when the moon was in the position

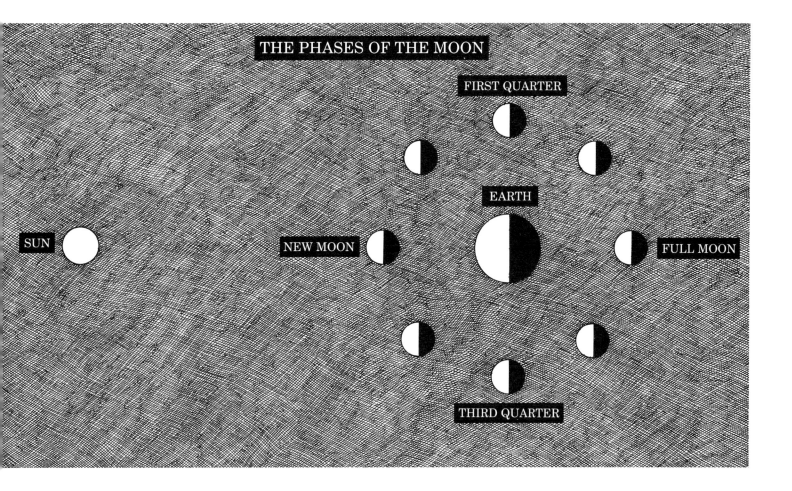

THE PHASES OF THE MOON

FIRST QUARTER

EARTH

SUN

NEW MOON

FULL MOON

THIRD QUARTER

shown at the far left, you would see no moonlight at all. The moon's illuminated side would be completely hidden from the earth. This phase is called the "new moon." If you looked into the sky at night when the moon was in the position shown at the far right, you would see a "full moon." The moon's illuminated side would be completely visible from the earth.

Between the time the moon is "new" and the time it is full, you can see more and more of its illuminated side each night. The moon thus appears to be growing, or *waxing*. As the moon moves from its full position back to the "new" position, it appears to be getting smaller, or *waning*. The whole cycle from new moon to full moon and back is called the *lunar cycle*.

ANCIENT CALENDARS

After noticing the relationship between the changing seasons and the sun, people tried to find ways to divide up the seasons. One logical way to do this was to use the lunar cycle, since each season could be divided into several lunar cycles, or months. However, 12 lunar months did not add up to one solar year. This was the big problem to be solved by the makers of early lunar calendars.

The ancient Babylonians tried to solve the problem by creating a 19-year cycle of changing months to correct the difference between the lunar cycles and the solar year. Seven of the years on the Babylonian calendar had 13 months and the other 12 years had 12 months. This system has been called the *Metonic cycle* after the Babylonian astronomer Meton, who lived in about 430 B.C. While this solved the problem, the Metonic calendar was too complicated for everyday use.

Life in ancient Egypt depended on the great Nile River. Without it, the Egyptians would have had no water to irrigate their crops. The river also became a highway for boats carrying trade goods and construction materials for the great pyramids and temples. It is not surprising, then, that it was used to create the Egyptian calendar.

Egyptians had discovered that the length of a year was 365 days. They also noticed that the Nile rose and fell each season at about the same time. Their earliest calendar was a simple vertical scale marked on a pole set into the riverbank. Each year the flood level was recorded on the pole.

However, this "nilometer" was not very accurate. So as early as 4221 B.C., the Egyptians had devised a better calendar. It had 12 months of 30 days each, with 5 days added onto the end of each year to bring the total to 365 days.

Because the solar year is not exactly 365 days, the Egyptian calendar gradually got ahead of the actual year. The Egyptian year became a "wandering year," in which each month moved through the seasons every 1460 years!

Although the Egyptian government required its people to use the solar calendar, the lunar cycle was still used by the Egyptians and other Middle Eastern cultures for religious purposes. The Jewish year, for instance, consists of 12 months of 29 or 30 days, making a total of 354 days. To make up for the extra days not included at the end of each year, the Jewish calendar adds leap years in which a whole month is added. These leap years occur in the 3rd, 6th, 8th, 11th, 14th, 17th, and 19th years of the Metonic cycle. Other adjustments sometimes have to be made to make sure that religious holidays fall at the proper time. For example, the spring holiday, Passover, must always occur after the vernal equinox.

After the Romans conquered Egypt, they recognized that the Egyptian calendar was superior to their own, and in 46 B.C. the Emperor Julius Caesar adopted it for use throughout the Empire. From then on, it became known as the Julian calendar.

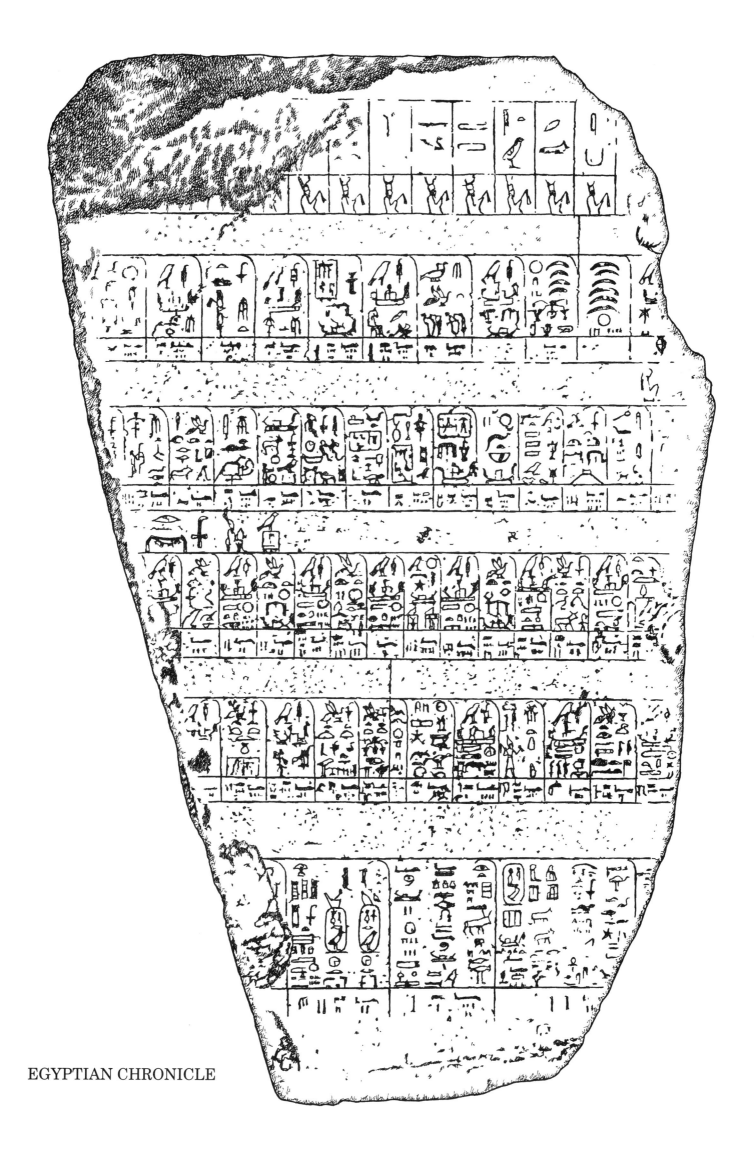

EGYPTIAN CHRONICLE

THE MEDIEVAL CALENDAR

By the Middle Ages, the European calendar looked much like the one we use today. In these pages from a medieval calendar, each month is illustrated with its own rural activity. Put together, the months make up a prayer book known as a *book of hours*, which was made for a French nobleman, Jean, Duc de Berry, in the early 1400s. Here we see February, March, August, and November. The semicircle above each picture shows the sun moving across the sky and the signs of the zodiac for that month.

The official calendar, on which the Duc de Berry's book of hours was based, was the Julian calendar that Julius Caesar had established many hundreds of years before. However, there was a problem with this calendar. By the 16th century, it was well over a week out of sequence with the actual solar year. When Julius Caesar had adopted it, he had added an extra day every four years — a *leap year*. However, the solar year is actually 365¼ days and 11 minutes long. These minutes had added up to many days by the 16th century.

This would not have created any difficulty except for the fact that the date of Easter, one of the Church's most important festivals, followed the solar year. Easter was always celebrated the first Sunday after the appearance of the first full moon after the vernal equinox. Because the Julian calendar had missed 11 minutes each year for hundreds of years, the vernal equinox was now occurring on March 11th, rather than March 21st. If something was not done, Easter would eventually fall on the same date as Christmas!

In 1545, Pope Gregory XIII called the Church leaders together at the Council of Trent, and set up a new calendar now known as the Gregorian calendar. Ten days were omitted. October 5th became October 15th. Three leap years were to be dropped in four centuries. This change left the Gregorian year about 25 seconds longer than the solar year, which was not bad, compared to the Julian calendar.

Although this solved the problem of Easter and Christmas, some European countries were slow to adopt the new calendar. England, for instance, used the Julian calendar until 1752. They switched to the Gregorian calendar, which is still used today.

JANUS

THE MONTHS OF THE YEAR

The names of the months used in most European countries and in North America come to us from the Julian calendar. The ones shown below are the English versions.

January, the first month of the year, is named for the Roman god Janus. He was the two-headed god of beginnings, endings and gates.

February, the second month of the year, was originally the last month. *Februarius* comes from the Latin word meaning "to purify." During the last month of the year, the Romans purified themselves to get ready for the festivals of the coming new year.

March, the third month of the year, was originally the first month. When Julius Caesar revised the calendar in the 1st century B.C., it became the third month. It is named in honour of Mars, the Roman god of war.

April, the fourth month of the year, is named for Aprilis, the Latin word meaning "to open."

May, the fifth month, is named for Maia, the Roman goddess of spring.

June, the sixth month, is named for the Roman goddess Juno. She was the wife of Zeus and the goddess of marriage.

July, the seventh month of the year, originally the fifth month, was called *Quintilis* — meaning "fifth." When Julius Caesar revised the calendar, he rather immodestly named this month after himself!

August, the eighth month, was named by the Romans for another emperor — Augustus.

September, the ninth month of the year, was originally the seventh month. Its name comes from the Latin word *septem*, meaning "seven."

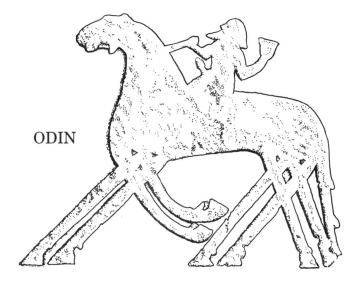

ODIN

October, the tenth month, was originally the eighth month and gets its name from the Latin word for "eight." The Roman Senate tried to change the name to "Antoninus," but the people kept calling it October.

November, the eleventh month, was originally the ninth month. Its name comes from the Latin *novem*, for "nine."

December, the twelfth month of the year, was originally the tenth month. *Decem* is the Latin word for "ten."

THE DAYS OF THE WEEK

While most European countries take the names of their months from the Julian calendar, the names of the days of the week are quite different from country to country. In the English-speaking world, the names of most days come from Anglo-Saxon and Old Norse traditions.

Sunday, the first day of the week, is named in honor of the sun, which was sacred to the people of northern Europe.

Monday, or moon-day, the second day of the week, honors the moon.

Tuesday is named for Tiu or Tyr, the Norse god of war.

Wednesday is named for Woden or Odin, the chief god in Norse mythology.

Thursday is named for Thor, the Norse god of thunder.

Friday comes from the Anglo-Saxon Frigg's day. Frigg was the Norse goddess of love.

Saturday, the seventh day of the week, is the only day that still has a Roman name. It is named for Saturn, the Roman god of the harvest.

MAYAN HIEROGLYPH

AZTEC AND MAYAN CALENDARS

As European timekeeping systems were developing during the Middle Ages, cultures unknown to them were using other ways of keeping track of time.

The Aztec and Maya peoples of Central America were accomplished astronomers and timekeepers. Central to their religion were the Four Ages, or multiple creations of the world. The present world was seen as one age, which was the sum of the four previous ages. The passage of time was thought to be a movement through the ages. The Aztec Sun Stone from Tenochtitlan expresses the idea of five ages in one.

The Maya were very interested in floods and eclipses. They developed advanced systems of mathematics and astronomy so they could predict when floods and eclipses would occur.

The Mayan calendar consisted of a 20-day week, or *ninal*. The choice of the 20 days was based on the 20 digits (fingers and toes) of the human body. Each of these days was given a hieroglyphic symbol.

AZTEC SUN STONE

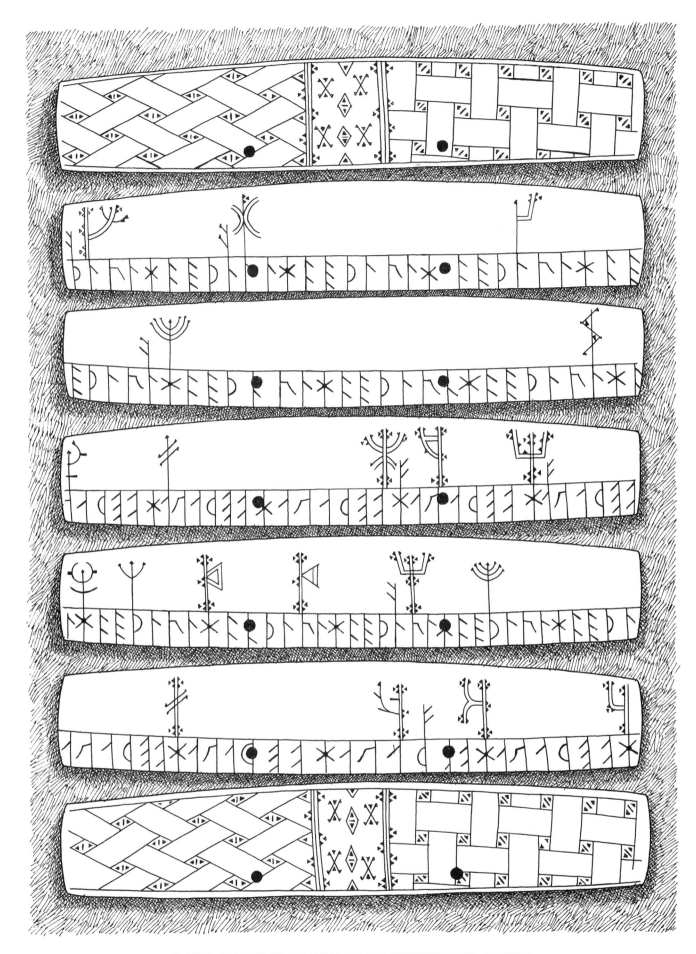

LAPP CALENDAR MADE OF REINDEER BONE

STRING CALENDAR
FROM SUMATRA

SIMPLE CALENDARS

While heads of state and Church leaders held long discussions to create proper calendars for the more complex societies of the world, smaller cultures made simple calendars that met their needs.

The Lapp, or Sami, people of northern Scandinavia spent most of their time herding reindeer. Their calendars were portable ones made from plates of reindeer bone tied together with thongs. The seven days of the week were symbolized by *runes* (ancient letters). Holidays were depicted with more elaborate ornaments.

The rural people of Sumatra in Indonesia created a simple string calendar to mark the passing of days in a lunar month. Each day was recorded by threading a string through one of 30 holes in a wooden plaque.

GNOMON

DIAL

S

PRIMITIVE SUNDIAL

30

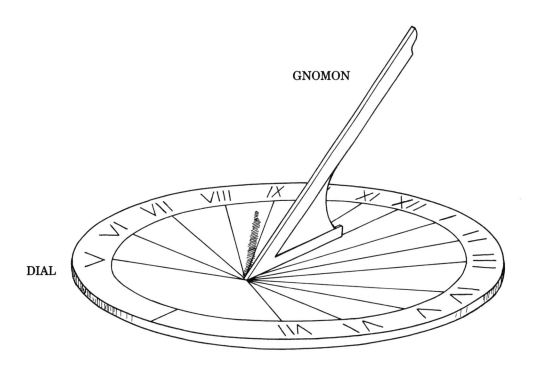

GNOMON

DIAL

HORIZONTAL SUNDIAL

SUNDIALS

The first two divisions of time that ancient peoples likely recognized were night and day. They would also have noticed that the sun came up over the eastern horizon, and rose and set again below the western horizon. As the sun moved, they would have observed that the shadows cast by trees, rocks and their own bodies were long in the morning, short at midday and long again in the evening. To tell time, they may at first have made a mark in the dirt to indicate the position of a tree's shadow at noon. The first sundial was likely just a stick placed upright in the ground with a few stones positioned in a semicircle around it.

Eventually, it was discovered that the shadow cast by a *gnomon,* or sundial pole, slanted at the same angle as the earth's axis and remained constant regardless of the season. After this discovery was made, people were able to construct much more accurate sundials. The slant principle is used in the garden sundials we are familiar with today.

For perhaps as many as 20 centuries, the sundial was the most commonly used timekeeping device. Even after mechanical clocks were invented, men could be seen setting their watches by the noon marking of the sundial in the town square.

Structures for observing the movement of the heavenly bodies have been found among the remains of many ancient civilizations. The great megalithic circle, Stonehenge, begun more than 4,000 years ago in southern England, was once thought to have been a Druid temple. Archeologists now believe it was built as an astronomical observatory. Other stone formations, such as the large Medicine Wheel constructed by native Americans in Wyoming, were probably large clocks and observatories.

Many early stone structures marked the *summer solstice* of June 21 or 22, the day of the year when shadows are the shortest. Special celebrations were often held on this day.

While these great observatories and timekeepers were being perfected, humbler sun-and-shadow devices were being developed for calculating the hours of the day. By the 10th century B.C., the Egyptians were using a T-shaped "time stick." It consisted of one vertical stick and one crossbar. The names of five

hours were written in hieroglyphics on the stick. In the morning, the time stick was placed so that it faced east. The shadow of the crossbar would then fall across the stick and move toward the crossbar until noon. To mark the afternoon hours, the time stick was turned to face west.

The Greeks and Romans also used sun and shadow to tell time. In 450 B.C., the historian Herodotus wrote that it was the Babylonians who taught the Greeks about the *gnomon*, or sundial pole, and about dividing the day into 12 parts. After their conquest of Egypt, the Romans brought back a giant obelisk, marked with hieroglyphics, and placed it in a square to serve as a gnomon for a great sundial. In 200 B.C., the Roman playwright Plautus cursed "... the wretch who first ... set a sundial in the marketplace to chop my day into pieces."

ANGEL WITH SUNDIAL,
CHARTRES CATHEDRAL

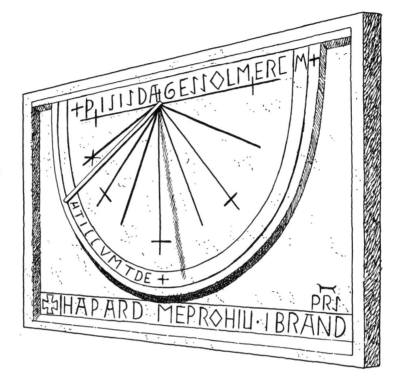

SUNDIAL IN WALL OF
KIRKDALE CHURCH

MEDIEVAL SUNDIALS

During the Middle Ages, sundials were built into the walls of churches. The sundial was placed so it faced south. The gnomon was placed in the dial at an angle based on the sundial's latitude. Time was told by the angle of the shadow, which moved around the dial like the hands of a modern clock.

The sundial on Kirkdale Church in Yorkshire was constructed in 1060. It divided the day into 8 daylight "tides" (Anglo-Saxon hours), rather than 12.

Several hundred miles south, at Chartres in France, an angel built into the cathedral wall holds a vertical sundial that divides the day into 12 hours.

In the Middle Ages, time was often viewed as a symbol of mortality. Timepieces on churches were therefore frequently accompanied by comments about the end of time when death would no longer exist. These words, for instance, were written into the grand calendar at Bergiers in France: "And the angel of judgement will proclaim an end to time."

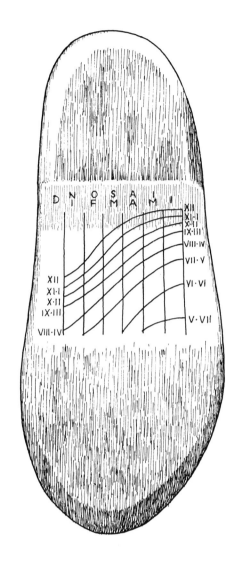

CLOG SUNDIAL

UNUSUAL SUNDIALS

In northern Europe, peasants used sundials carved into the bottoms of their wooden clogs. To tell the time, a peasant would take off his shoe and stand it up facing the sun. The hour was told by the shadow the heel cast on the dial!

Another medieval European folk device for telling time was the "hand dial." The gnomon on this simple sundial was just a stick. It was held by the thumb at an angle. To tell the morning hours, the gnomon was held in the left hand and the left hand was held horizontal to the earth, pointing west. In the afternoon, the gnomon was held in the right hand and the right hand pointed east. A very inexpensive watch!

Long after the invention of mechanical clocks had made sundials a thing of the past, people still made sundials for fun. In the 19th century, sun cannons were even made. They consisted of a sundial and a small cannon. A magnifying glass was mounted above the cannon at such an angle that when the sun passed at noon, the glass would focus the sun's light onto the cannon's fuse.

The result — BANG!

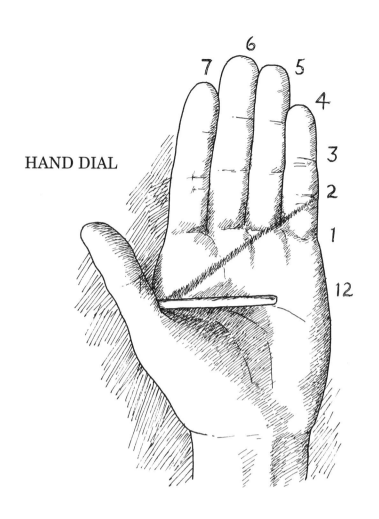

HAND DIAL

SUN CANNON

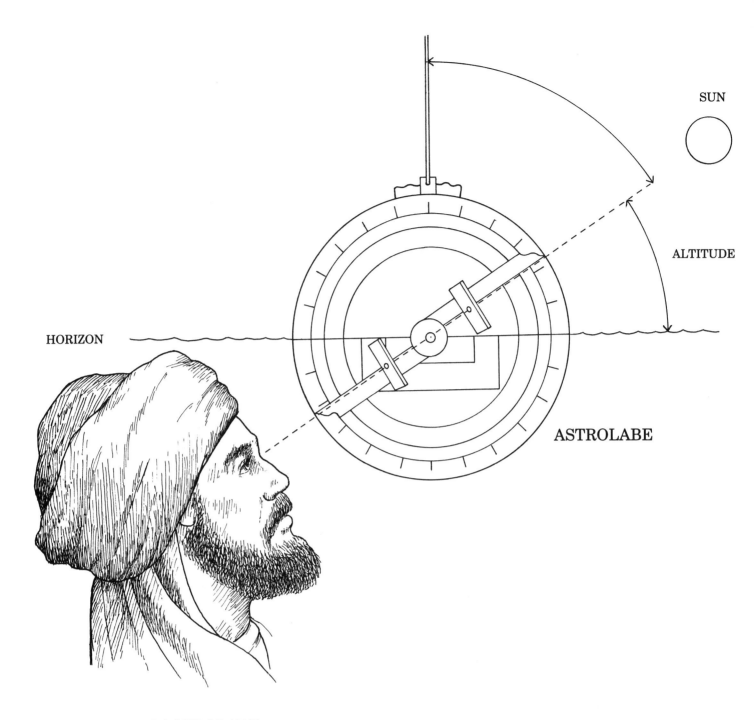

SUN

ALTITUDE

HORIZON

ASTROLABE

THE ASTROLABE

The astrolabe was the high technology of the Middle Ages. It was invented by Arabic researchers and craftsmen in about 100 A.D. Using this instrument, a person could determine the latitude and the time of day or night. The astrolabe was brought to western Europe during the Middle Ages and was used by navigators until the middle of the 18th century.

Astrolabes are constructed around a metal disc. The arm extending from the center of this disc to its edge is used to determine the altitude of the sun. A second, open dial called a *rete* shows the position of the brightest stars. Once the altitude of the sun is determined, the rete is rotated to the proper position to indicate the time.

The astrolabe was small and portable. It is often considered to have been the first watch.

FRONT VIEW

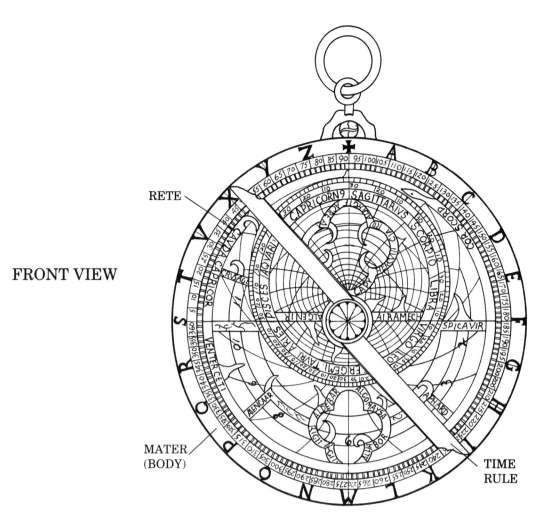

RETE

MATER
(BODY)

TIME
RULE

REAR VIEW

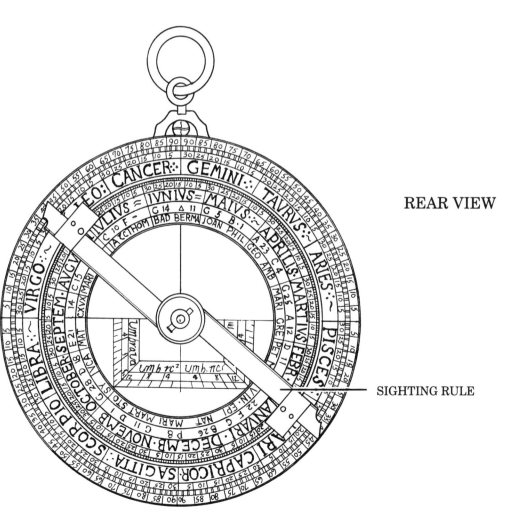

SIGHTING RULE

43

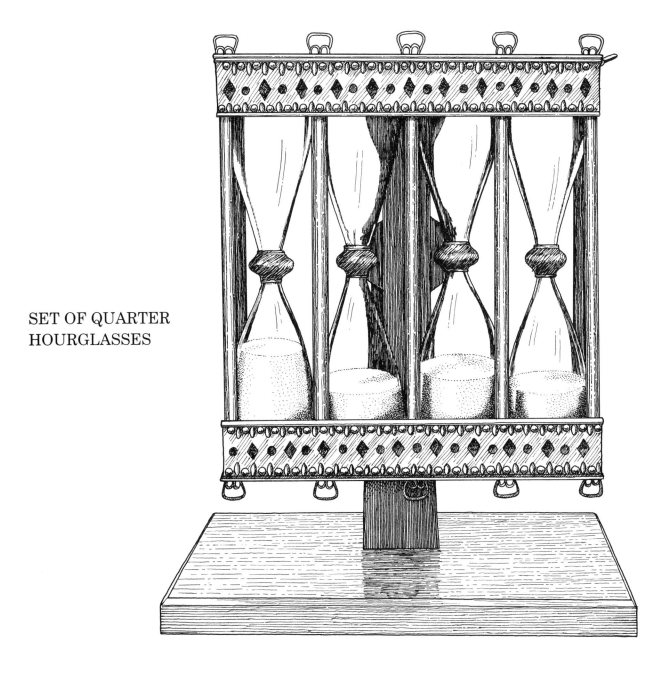

SET OF QUARTER
HOURGLASSES

UNUSUAL TIMEKEEPERS

Hourglasses were widely used before the invention of the mechanical clock. They were especially useful for measuring short periods of time. A set amount of sand was put into the bottom of a closed-in glass that was very narrow in the middle. The glass was then turned upside down, and the sand would start to run slowly through the narrow middle part to the other end of the glass. Since the sand would always take the same amount of time to run through, it was an accurate measure of time. Some hourglasses were mounted in sets of

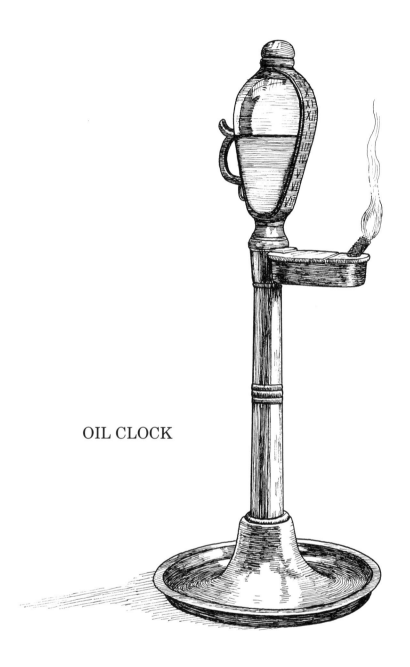

OIL CLOCK

four to divide an hour into quarters. People still use hourglasses today to measure the amount of time it takes to boil an egg.

Oil clocks have been used in many cultures. One kind of oil clock, used in 18th-century Germany, was an oil lamp whose glass oil reservoir was marked from top to bottom with the hours from 8:00 p.m. to 7:00 a.m. If you lit the wick at 8:00 p.m., the oil would start to burn down, taking exactly one hour to go from the 8:00 p.m. marker to the 9:00 p.m. marker. This clock was also "self-illuminating"!

WATER CLOCKS

Sundials were reliable timekeepers, but they had their limitations: they could not be used after sunset, they did not work on cloudy days and they could not be used indoors. To overcome these problems, water clocks were developed.

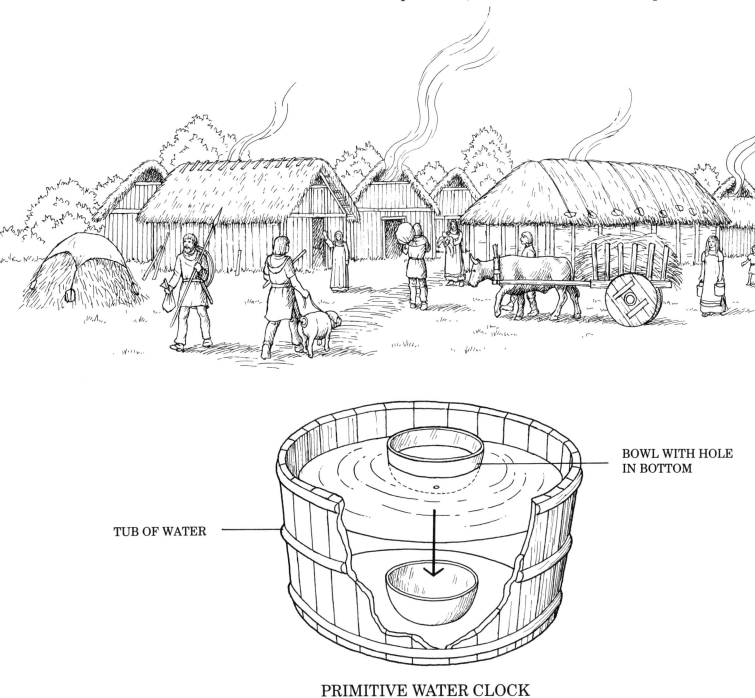

TUB OF WATER

BOWL WITH HOLE
IN BOTTOM

PRIMITIVE WATER CLOCK

One of the earliest water clocks was simply a bowl with a small hole in the bottom. The bowl was placed in a tub, where it would float. As water leaked into the bowl through the hole, the bowl would sink. When it hit bottom, the person on watch would empty the bowl and put it back on the water's surface. The length of time it took the bowl to sink would be one unit of time. By keeping track of the number of times the bowl sank, the person on watch could tell how many units of time had past.

Even in this century sailors on Indonesian ships have used water clocks — made from coconut shells — to keep time at sea.

EGYPTIAN WATER CLOCK

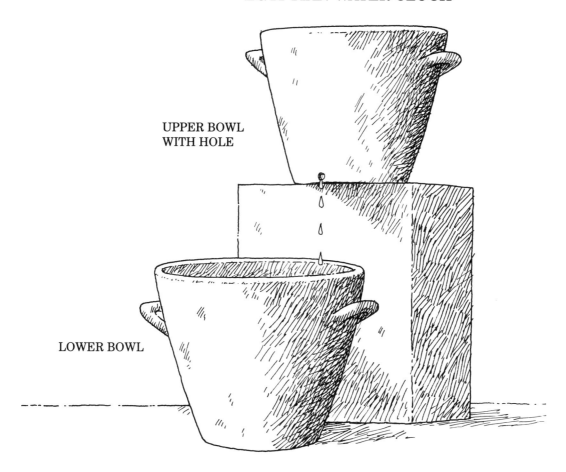

UPPER BOWL
WITH HOLE

LOWER BOWL

The first truly accurate water clock was probably invented by the Egyptians. It was called a *clepsydra* and consisted of a water-filled jar with a small hole in the bottom and another jar with a time scale marked up the side. The water-filled jar was placed above the other one, and the water would drip into the empty jar at a steady rate.

Simple water clocks such as these were used in Greek and Roman courts. Lawyers were given a full container of water, which represented the time they had to make their arguments. The container held about 30 gallons (about 110 liters) and took about 20 minutes to empty — at which point a speaker's time had "run out."

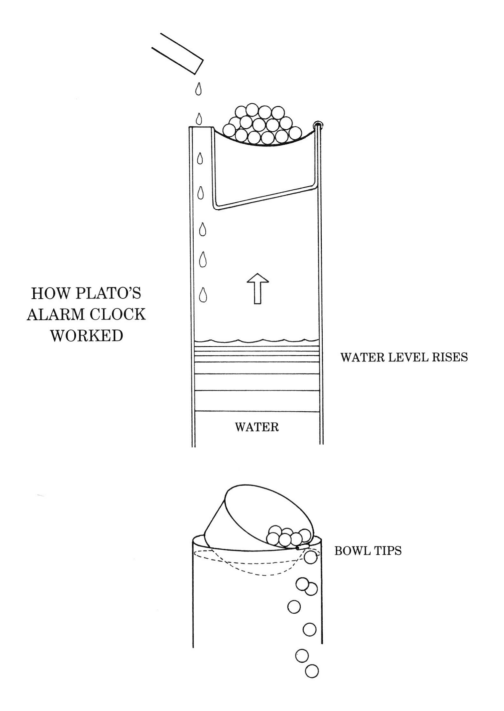

HOW PLATO'S
ALARM CLOCK
WORKED

WATER LEVEL RISES

WATER

BOWL TIPS

The famous Greek philosopher and teacher Plato may have invented the first alarm clock — for the purpose of waking up his students at the Academy in Athens! Water dripped from a large container into a graded cylinder, at the top of which sat a hinged bowl filled with lead balls. When the water reached the top of the cylinder, it caused the bowl to overturn, and the lead balls spilled out onto a large copper plate with a clatter!

The science and technology for constructing water clocks was well known in the Arab world. In the fifth century A.D., a wonderful ornamental clock was built at Ghaza. It included moving statues of the sun god and Hercules and doors that opened and closed.

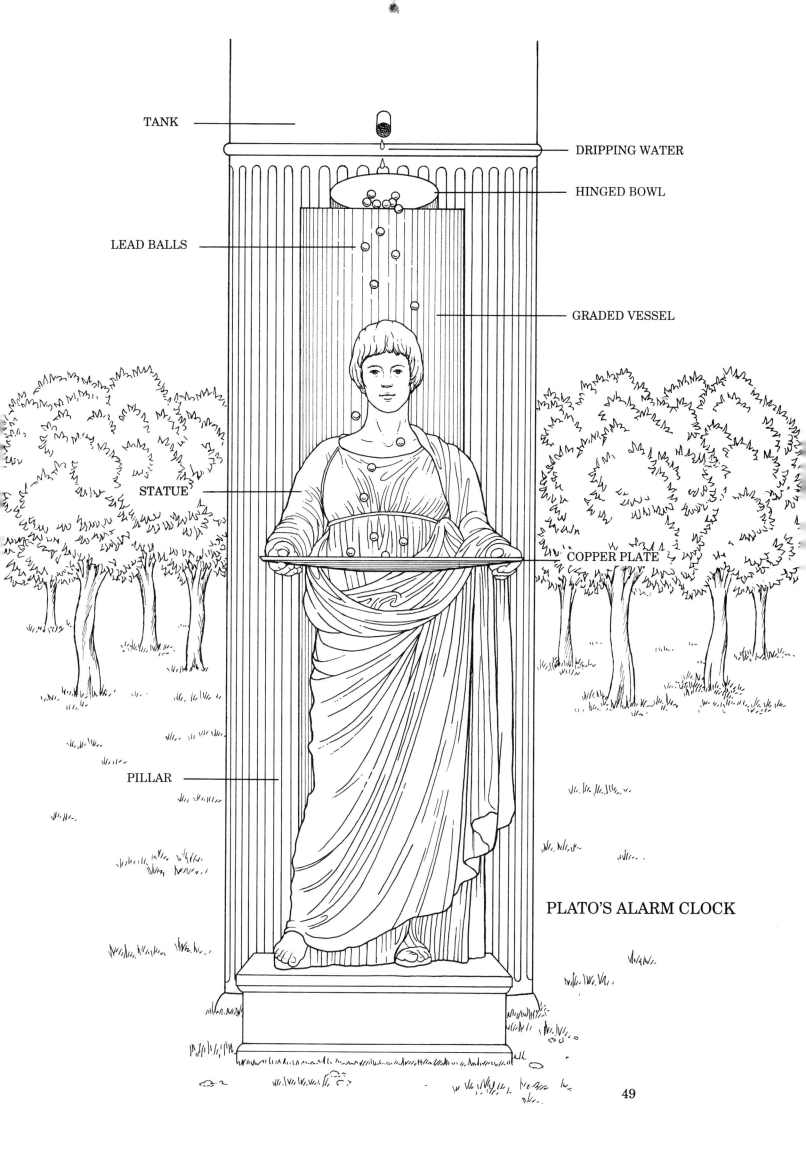

TANK

DRIPPING WATER

HINGED BOWL

LEAD BALLS

GRADED VESSEL

STATUE

COPPER PLATE

PILLAR

PLATO'S ALARM CLOCK

49

ARABIC WATER CLOCK WITH SIGNS OF THE ZODIAC

Among the most famous water clocks was the giant one at the east gate of the Great Mosque in Damascus. It created an amazing spectacle, dropping balls, ringing bells and lighting oil lamps to mark each hour of the day and night. Eleven men working full-time were required to maintain this great clock.

In about 1200 A.D., the renowned clockmaker Ismaeel al-Jazari wrote a book called *The Science of Ingenious Mechanisms*. In it he described the construction of ten ornamental water clocks. Much of this knowledge was lost when the Mongols captured Baghdad in 1258.

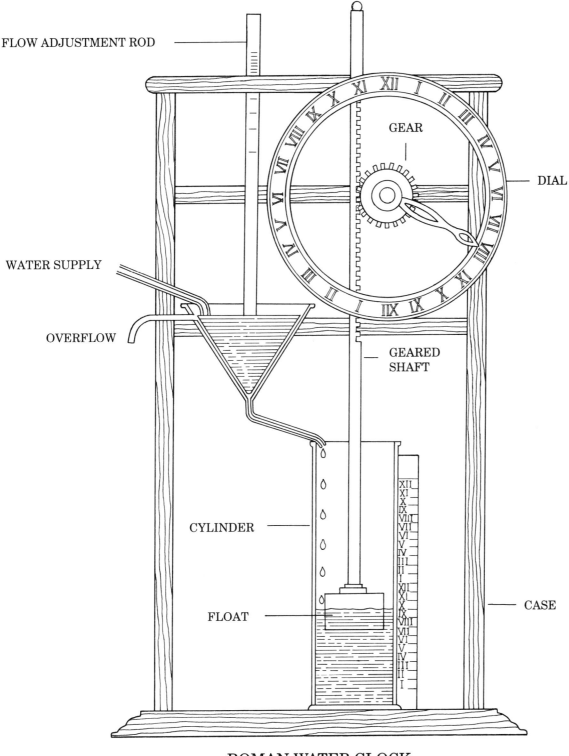

FLOW ADJUSTMENT ROD

GEAR

DIAL

WATER SUPPLY

OVERFLOW

GEARED
SHAFT

CYLINDER

CASE

FLOAT

ROMAN WATER CLOCK

Using gears and floats, the Romans turned the clepsydra into a 24-hour instrument with a hand similar to those on the clocks we know today. As you can see from the illustration, water flows into a conical reservoir and drips through a small tube in the bottom. The water rises in the cylinder, which causes the float to rise. The geared shaft attached to the float then rises, causing the round gear attached to the hand to turn and mark the hours. The flow of water into the cylinder can be adjusted by raising or lowering the flow adjustment rod.

ARMILLARY SPHERE

CELESTIAL GLOBE

DRIVE AND
ESCAPEMENT

DISPLAY

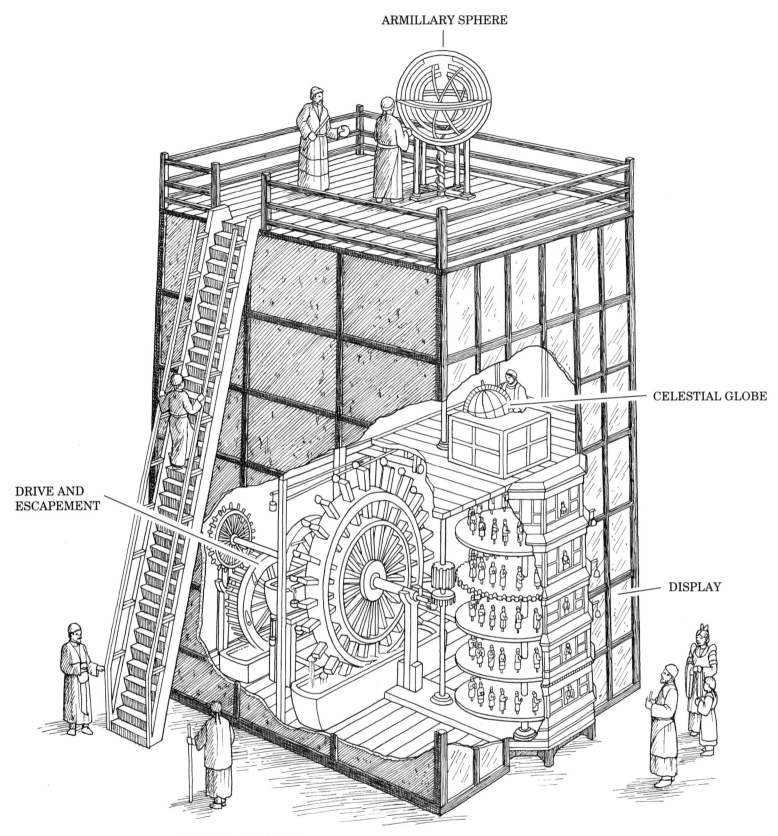

CHINESE WATER-WHEEL CLOCK

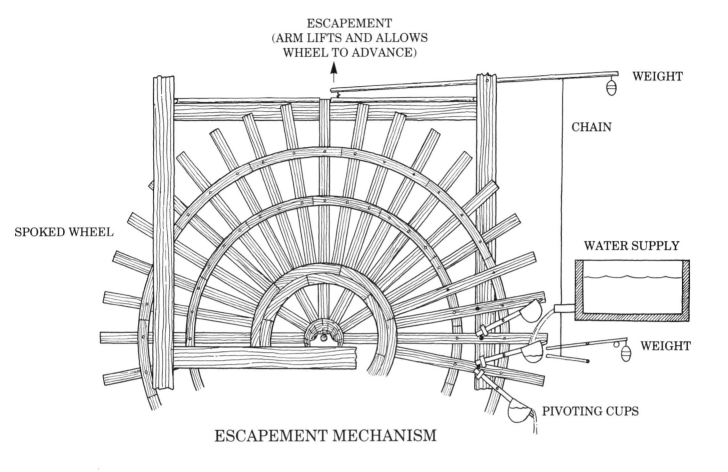

ESCAPEMENT
(ARM LIFTS AND ALLOWS
WHEEL TO ADVANCE)

WEIGHT

CHAIN

SPOKED WHEEL

WATER SUPPLY

WEIGHT

PIVOTING CUPS

ESCAPEMENT MECHANISM

The clepsydra continued to be used in this form in Europe long after the collapse of the Roman Empire. In the Orient, however, *horologists*, or clockmakers, at the court of the Chinese emperor were beginning to construct clocks that had some of the features of later mechanical clocks. Between the 8th and 11th centuries A.D., the Chinese built a clock powered by a wheel with cups of equal weight and capacity placed around the rim. When a cup had filled with water, it tripped a lever that released it, permitting the next cup to take its place. This process of controlled holding back and letting go was called the *escapement*. In this case, the escapement allowed the wheel to turn in equal increments, each of which represented one unit of time. Traveling merchants brought the technology to Europe, where it was eagerly accepted. By the early 13th century in Germany, clockmakers were so numerous that they had formed a guild, or society, of clockmakers.

Water clocks had their limitations, though: they did not keep completely accurate time, and they tended to freeze during the harsh European winters!

53

THE MONASTIC CLOCK

Following the collapse of the Roman Empire, the medieval church tried to bring order and stability out of the resulting confusion. One of the ways they did this was to set up monasteries, where monks and other religious people could live lives of discipline and prayer.

The Rule of St. Benedict, which was followed in all the monasteries belonging to the Benedictine order, divided the day into seven periods of prayer. In the seventh century, Pope Sabinianas decreed that the bells of the monasteries

be rung seven times every 24 hours. These divisions of the day were known as the "canonical hours." Water clocks and, later, mechanical clocks powered by falling weights were used to determine when those bells should be rung. The old French children's rhyme "Frère Jacques" (Brother John) refers to the ringing of the monastery bells: "Are you sleeping, Are you sleeping, Brother John, Brother John? Morning bells are ringing, morning bells are ringing. Ding, dang, dong, ding, dang, dong."

MECHANICAL CLOCKS

The first mechanical clock was powered by a weight attached to a cord wound around a cylinder. The *verge escapement*, with an *oscillating foliot bar*, was used to hold and release the power of the falling weight. It was developed in the first half of the 14th century. No one knows for certain who invented it, but the inventor may have been the Englishman Richard of Wallingford or the renowned Italian physician and astronomer Giovanni Di Dondi. Without this device, mechanical clocks could never have been built.

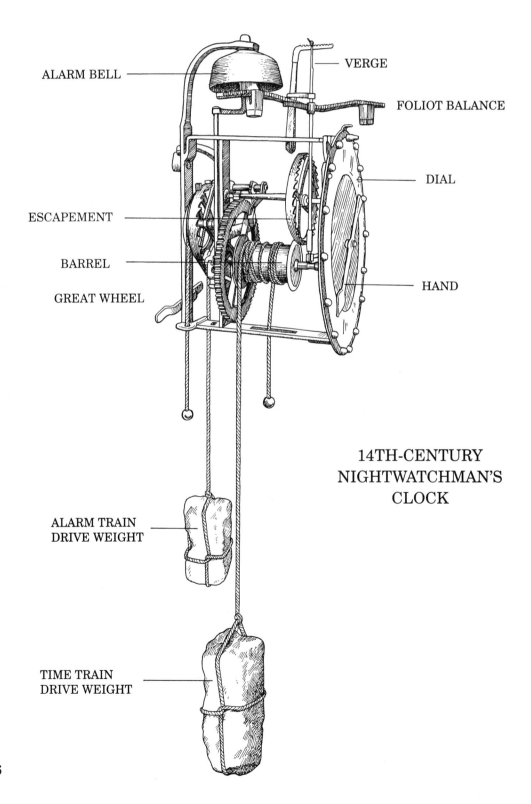

ALARM BELL

VERGE

FOLIOT BALANCE

DIAL

ESCAPEMENT

BARREL

GREAT WHEEL

HAND

14TH-CENTURY
NIGHTWATCHMAN'S
CLOCK

ALARM TRAIN
DRIVE WEIGHT

TIME TRAIN
DRIVE WEIGHT

VERGE AND FOLIOT ESCAPEMENT

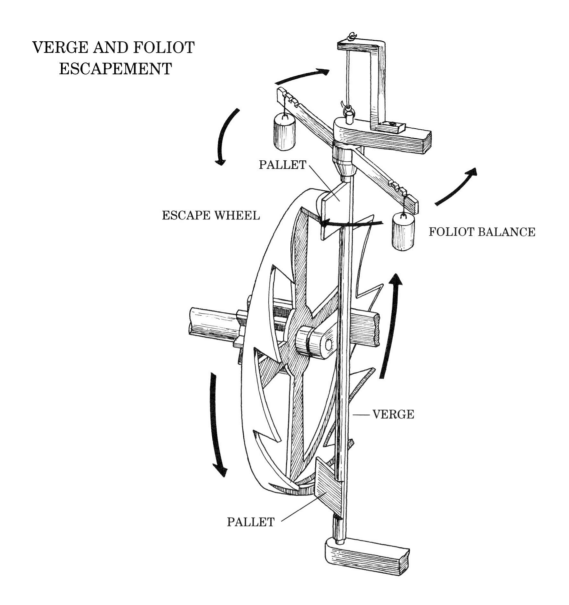

PALLET

ESCAPE WHEEL

FOLIOT BALANCE

VERGE

PALLET

This weight-driven clock with a *verge and foliot escapement* works like this: The weight drives the barrel with the great wheel, which in turn is connected by a spindle to the *escape wheel*. As this toothed wheel turns, its motion is interrupted at regular intervals by two *pallets*. The pallets are set at right angles to each other on a rod called a verge. As the escape wheel turns, one of the pallets is pushed aside, causing the verge to turn and the *foliot balance* to turn. The foliot balance is stopped when the other pallet engages a tooth in the wheel. This escapement allows the hand, which is connected to the verge, to turn in equal increments.

JACQUEMARTS
RINGING BELLS

TOWN CLOCKS

With the rise of cities in 14th-century Europe, the demand for skilled clock-makers increased. Town clocks, which regulated the workday, the markets and holidays, were placed prominently in public places. These tower clocks were expensive to build and became symbols of urban prosperity and civic pride. Powerful princes would lend their clockmakers to each other as gifts.

These early clocks were not only timekeepers. They were extravagant visual displays, with angels trumpeting, cocks crowing, and kings and prophets marching out at the ringing of the hours.

MECHANICAL ROOSTER
FROM STRASBOURG

Scholars in the late Middle Ages developed mechanical devices that helped them make clocks more reliable. These devices also helped scholars in early Renaissance times to create elaborate mechanical displays known as *automata* (because they worked automatically). The parts of early mechanical clocks that struck the hour often took the form of *jacquemarts* (mechanical watchmen), who hit the bells with tiny hammers. The 14th-century clock on the cathedral at Strasbourg, France, even had a bellows-powered mechanical rooster that flapped its wings and crowed at noon!

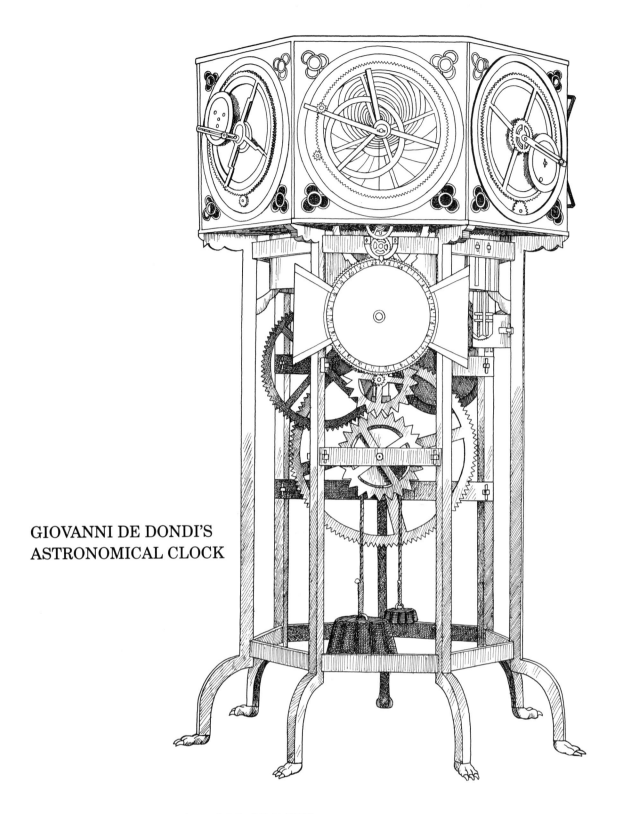

GIOVANNI DE DONDI'S ASTRONOMICAL CLOCK

ASTRONOMICAL CLOCKS

Astronomical clocks are elaborate mechanical devices that show not only the time of day but also the position of the moon, stars and planets. The earliest recorded astronomical clock was built by Richard of Wallingford. He began building the clock in 1327. After his death in 1336, the work was continued by Laurence de Stokes and William Walsham and completed in 1349.

Giovanni de Dondi spent 16 years building a clock that not only told the time but also followed the movements of the sun, the moon and the five known

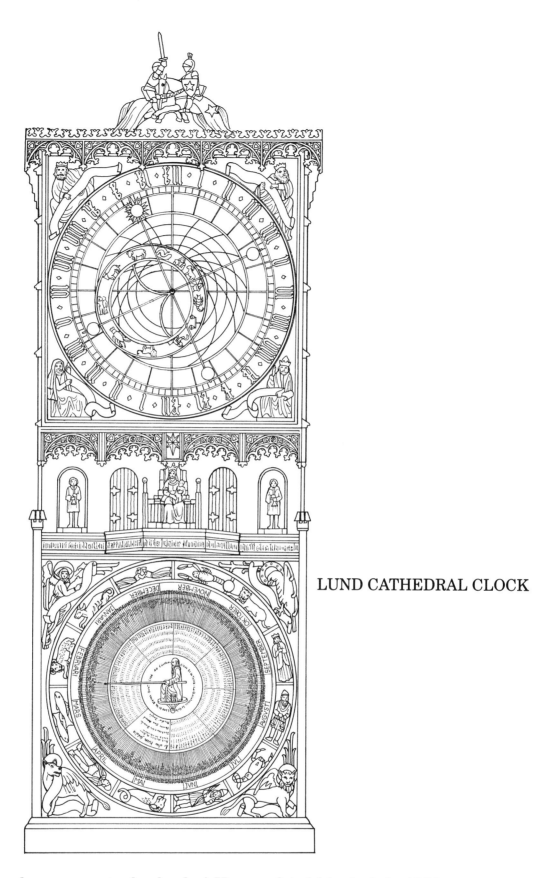

LUND CATHEDRAL CLOCK

planets, and served as a perpetual calendar! He completed his clock in 1364. Its elaborate gearing was a monumental technical achievement.

From the 14th to the 16th centuries, many public buildings in Europe were fitted with astronomical clocks. One of the most remarkable of these was the tall clock in the cathedral at Lund, Sweden. It was originally built in 1380. On its upper dial is a double outer 12-hour ring and an inner eccentric ring (an off-center ring) displaying the signs of the zodiac and indexes for the sun and the moon.

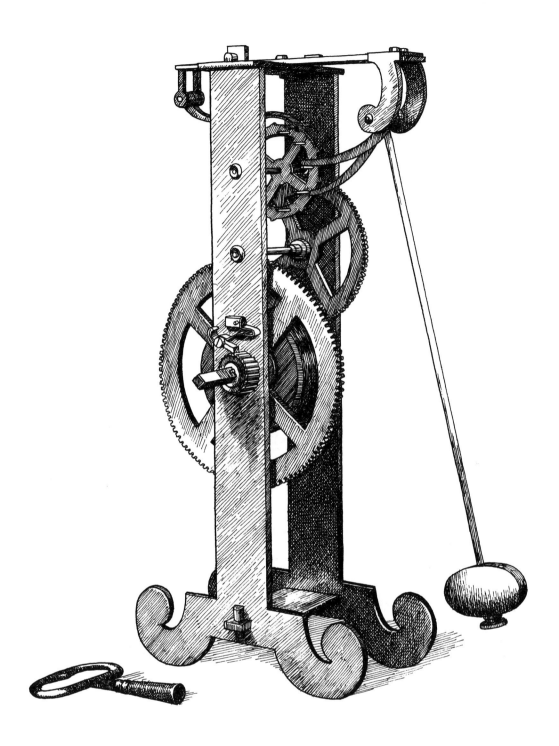

GALILEO'S PENDULUM

The Italian physicist Galileo discovered the principle of the *pendulum* while watching a hanging lamp swing back and forth. He noticed that no matter how wide the *arc,* or distance, of the swing was, the time, or *period*, that it took to return to its original position was always the same. Galileo believed that this principle could be used to regulate clocks. In 1637, he made drawings of pendulum devices that were later made into models.

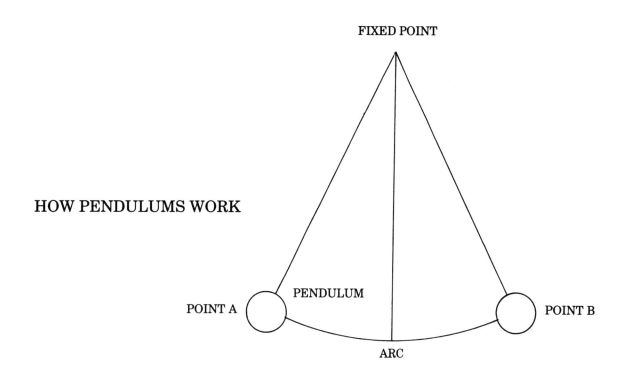

HOW PENDULUMS WORK

FIXED POINT

PENDULUM

POINT A

POINT B

ARC

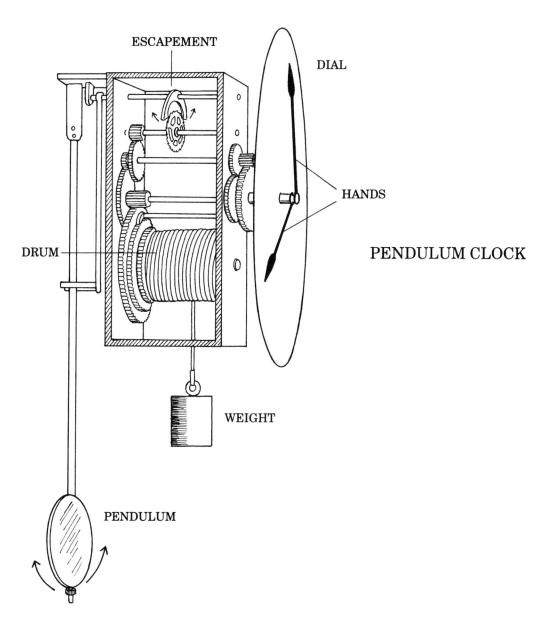

ESCAPEMENT

DIAL

HANDS

PENDULUM CLOCK

DRUM

WEIGHT

PENDULUM

Although Galileo was the first to have the idea of a clock with an escapement based on the swinging of a pendulum, it was Christian Huygens of the Netherlands who first applied the pendulum principle successfully to clocks. Huygens used a free-swinging pendulum on a cord as an escapement. This change increased the accuracy of mechanical clocks from an error of 15 *minutes* a day to an error of 8 to 10 *seconds* a day! Upright clocks employing the new device were constructed everywhere, and existing mechanical clocks were converted.

LUNAR DIAL FACE

Within a few years the Englishman Thomas Tompion was building and improving on the long-case clock, or grandfather clock. Among Tompion's clocks was one that he built for the National Observatory at Greenwich.

Grandfather clocks, whose weights and pendulum are enclosed in tall, wooden cases, have fascinated people ever since they were first built. Maybe this is because they seem to have personalities of their own. In the 19th century, many grandfather clocks were made with curious faces. One face marked off the 29½ days of a lunar month.

GRANDFATHER CLOCK

WATCHES

The weight-driven system worked well for large, stationary clocks, but it did not make them very portable. This was a problem for kings, nobles and, later, businessmen, who moved around frequently and wanted to take their timepieces with them. In about 1500, Peter Heinlein, a German locksmith, came up with a possible solution. Coiled springs had been used in locks since about 1400. Heinlein recognized the possibility of using a coiled steel or brass mainspring to power a clock.

Again the problem of an escapement arose. Since a mainspring becomes weaker as it winds down, it needs a device to keep its power constant. Clockmakers trying to solve this problem knew that the verge escapement and

CLOCK MECHANISM WITH MAINSPRING AND FUSÉE

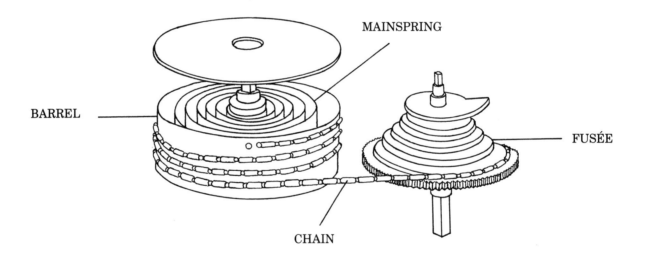

oscillating foliot bar would not work well in a timepiece that was constantly being shaken and moved about. So they had to figure out something else. After many years of effort and experimentation, two solutions were found — the *stackfreed* and the *fusée*.

The *stackfreed* consists of a snail-shaped disc and a stiff-arched spring. The pressure on the arched spring becomes less as the mainspring winds down. This maintains constant pressure to drive the clock.

The *fusée* is considered to be a better solution. It consists of a spiral cone with a fine cord of chain wound around it and attached to the mainspring. The varying diameter of the cone regulates the decreasing power of the mainspring as it winds down.

Early watches were rather thick and had metal covers with holes for viewing the numbers on the dial. Glass or "crystal" covers were not yet in use. Nor were watches always round. Peter Heinlein's earliest watches were known as "Nuremberg Eggs" because they were oval.

During the 17th and 18th centuries, however, many improvements in precision technology and miniaturization took place. These advances made it possible for thinner and lighter watches to be built.

EARLY WATCH WITH OPEN DIAL

One of the most important developments in precision was the invention of *jeweled bearings*. It had always been difficult to keep watches precise, because their metal parts would wear down with use. But in the early 18th century, Nicolas Facio, a Swiss immigrant working in London, discovered that rubies, harder and more durable than metal, could be pierced and used as bearings. These greatly reduced the friction and wear and tear on the moving parts in clocks and watches.

POCKET WATCH

For centuries, mechanical timepieces were luxuries that only the upper classes could afford. As commerce and technology expanded in the 1700s and 1800s, however, the number of middle-class consumers also grew. This new middle class increased the demand for inexpensive watches. The Swiss were the first to benefit from the boom. The small villages of the French-speaking Jura region became the center of the world watch industry. By 1885, the Swiss were exporting nearly 3 million watches a year. By 1913, the number had risen to 16 million. The Swiss dominated the watch industry until they were finally surpassed by the Japanese in the 1970s. In 1980, Japan exported 68 million watches to the rest of the world.

JAPANESE PORTABLE CLOCK

JAPANESE WATCHES

Early Japanese clocks were built with moveable dials. The numerals on these dials could be changed to allow for longer or shorter hours as the seasons changed. Later, during the economic and scientific reforms carried out by Emperor Meiji towards the end of the 19th century, the system of variable hours was changed to one of constant hours.

Pockets were never sewn into early Japanese clothing, so the Japanese wore portable clocks in small cases hung from their belts.

THE INDUSTRIAL AGE

In the 18th and 19th centuries, Europe and North America became more and more industrialized. As large groups of people began working together in offices and factories, there was a need for greater punctuality. So with the factory came the time clock. The worker punched in every morning and punched out every evening. The 19th-century workday was 12 hours long, and the work week lasted 6 days. The natural urges of rural life, such as taking off on a nice

spring day to go fishing, were discouraged. Irregular attendance at work and being late were looked upon almost as unfavorably as drunkenness.

While rigorous timekeeping was done in the interests of efficiency and productivity, it often created bored employees who therefore did not do their best work. Today many companies offer their workers "flex-time" — flexible work hours and workdays. It is now believed that people do their jobs more effectively if they are allowed more freedom in scheduling.

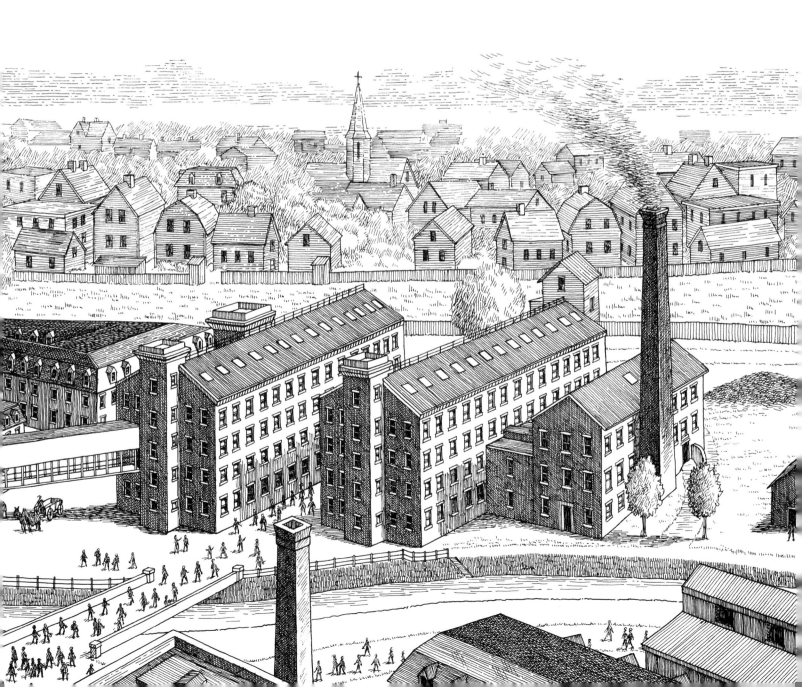

KEEPING TIME AT SEA

Sailors were probably among the first people to use the sun and stars to help them navigate. As soon as they ventured out of sight of land, the heavenly bodies were all they had to calculate their position. Determining *latitude* — their distance north or south of the equator — was quite simple. The navigator measured the height of the noon sun above the horizon. (At night he would use the North Star, Polaris, instead of the sun.) He then referred to previously calculated tables, called *ephemerals*, to find out where he was.

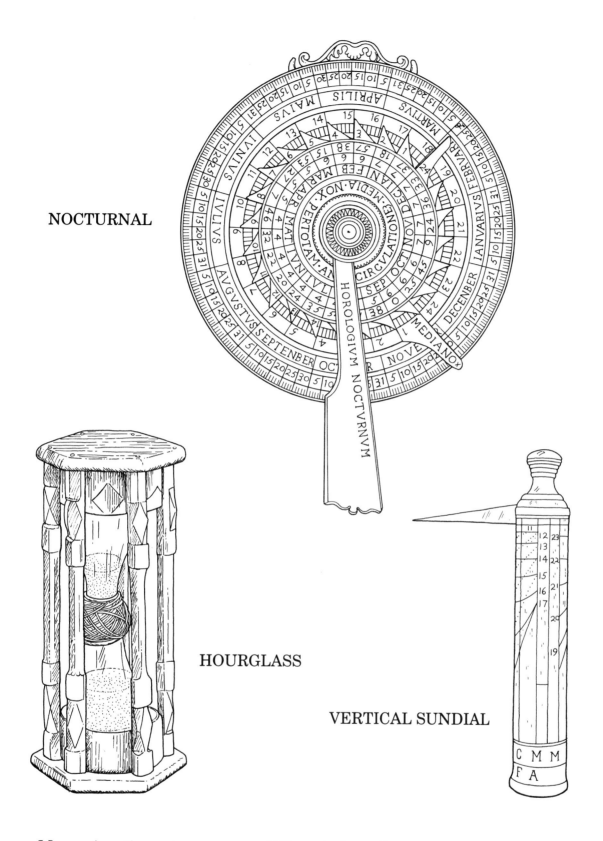

NOCTURNAL

HOURGLASS

VERTICAL SUNDIAL

Measuring *time* at sea was a different story. It was never very accurate. Sailors' timepieces included the *vertical sundial,* which could be adjusted for changes in latitude; the *hourglass,* to govern the four-hour watches; and the *nocturnal,* for calculating time by the movement of certain stars around the North Star at night. None of these devices was accurate enough for determining longitude, or east-west position.

THE GREENWICH OBSERVATORY

The Greenwich Observatory near London was founded in 1675 by King Charles II. Its original purpose was to improve navigation through the study of astronomy.

By the 17th century, Britain had become an important seafaring nation, but each year many of its ships were lost because of imprecise navigation. For centuries, navigators had been able to determine their latitude, but determining longitude was more difficult because it depended on calculating the position of the stars at a precise time. In 1713, the English Parliament offered a huge prize to anyone who could determine exact longitude at sea.

John Harrison, a young Yorkshire carpenter and clockmaker, was determined to win the "great prize." He knew that to determine longitude you needed to know your position in relation to the sun or stars at precise moments in time. So he set out to construct a portable clock capable of keeping time at sea and accurate to within two minutes in two months.

It took Harrison seven years to build his first *chronometer*. It was completed in 1735. The device was awkward-looking and weighed 72 pounds (about 32 kilograms) — but it was accurate. On a voyage to the West Indies and back to England, the chronometer was used to calculate the ship's position to within 26 miles (about 40 kilometers). Harrison spent the next 25 years developing more compact and reliable chronometers. He succeeded: his no. 4 chronometer was five inches (about 13 centimeters) in diameter and accurate to within a tenth of a second per day!

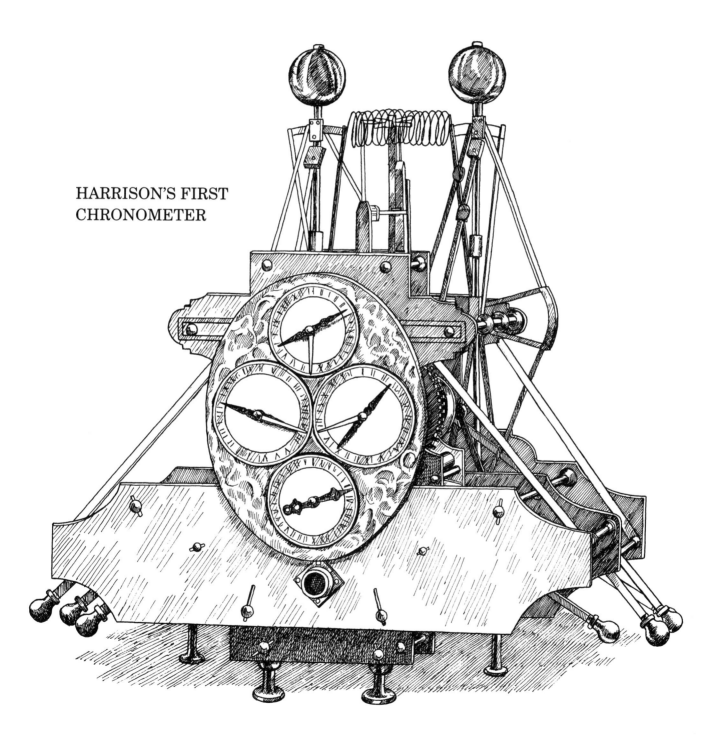

HARRISON'S FIRST
CHRONOMETER

STANDARD TIME

Until the latter half of the 19th century, the "correct time" for most people living in towns meant local "sun time." As one moves a few miles east or west, sun time changes. High noon occurs slightly earlier in one town than in its neighbor a little farther west. The difference in local time between New York and Chicago is a full hour.

The coming of the railroads brought the need for the time to be the same in many places at once. For a while each railroad line had its own "official time." Travelers would change their watches perhaps 20 times as they moved from one rail line to another across the continent. In 1883 the railroads agreed to a plan that divided North America into five time zones: Atlantic Standard Time (the Canadian Maritimes), Eastern Standard Time, Central Standard Time, Mountain Standard Time and Pacific Time.

G.W.R.R. TIMETABLE

		Read Down			Read Up	
448		**Lake Shore Limited**				449
12 49A	Dp	Oakville		Ar		9 14A
1 23A	▼	Windsor		▲		8 18A
2 01A	Ar	Lake City		Dp		7 11A
2 11A	Dp			Ar		7 01A
3 39A	↓	Riverdale		▲		5 28A
6 25A		New London				3 26A
7 56A	▼	Queenston				2 27A
8 38A	Ar	Tecumseh		Dp		1 02A

Connecting Services

TIME ZONES

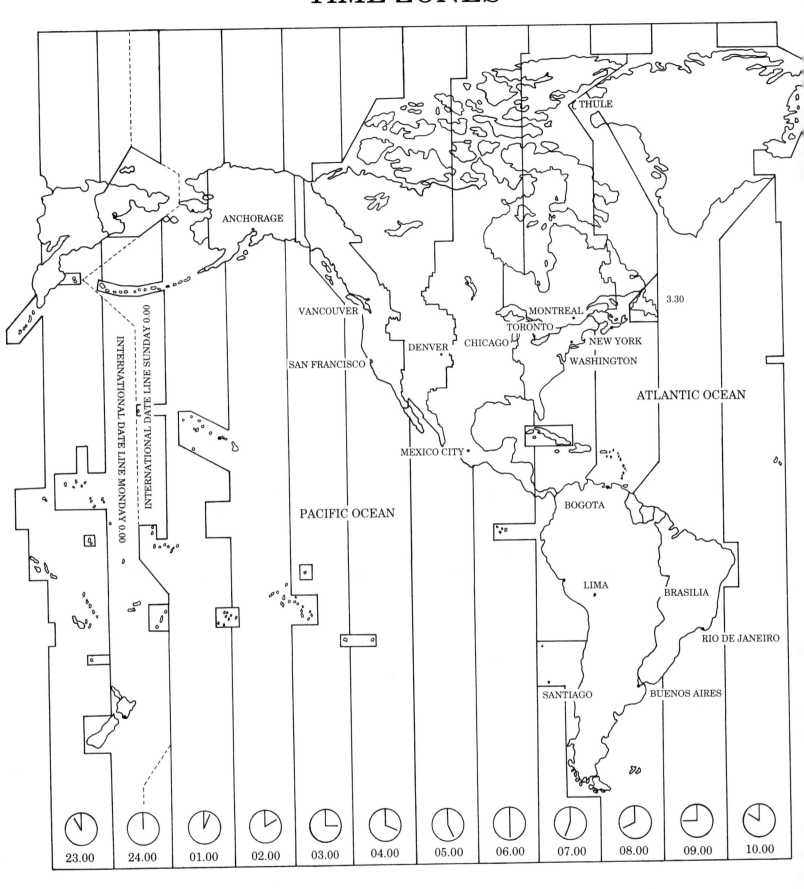

In 1884, an international conference of astronomers met in Washington to establish worldwide time zones. It was agreed that the starting point, or *prime meridian,* would pass through the Royal Observatory at Greenwich, England. The astronomers established 12 time zones to the east of Greenwich

AROUND THE WORLD

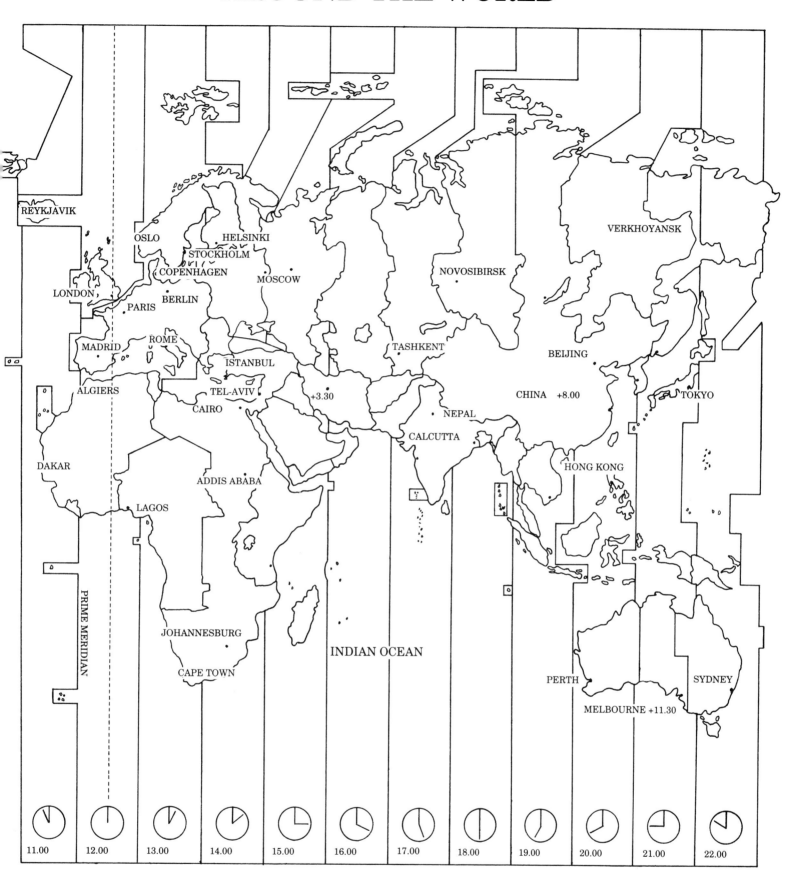

and 12 to the west. The 12th zone in each direction is a half-zone. The half-zones meet in the middle of the Pacific Ocean and are divided by the *International Date Line*. Travelers crossing the line from east to west lose a day. Those going from west to east gain a day.

MODERN TIME

The two-pendulum clock developed in 1921 by William H. Shortt took the development of the mechanical clock about as far as it could go. It reduced the effects of friction, but did not eliminate the problem completely.

In 1929, the American scientist Dr. Warren Morrison created the quartz clock. In this clock, an electric current was used to vibrate, or resonate, a quartz crystal hundreds of times per second. The internal friction of the quartz crystal was extremely low. The best quartz resonator clocks are accurate to within *one millisecond* per month.

QUARTZ WATCH

The earliest quartz clocks were large cabinet units that contained electronic equipment to regulate feedback and voltage. The invention of the integrated circuit made possible the miniaturization of these clocks. Today tiny batteries are used to power quartz crystal watches that are accurate to within one minute per year.

In 1957, the first electric watches were introduced. A tiny battery replaced the mainspring as a power source. In 1959, the balance wheel was replaced by a tuning fork. This development allowed watches to be accurate to within one minute per month.

The earliest quartz watches had dials with hands that looked exactly like the ones on mechanical clocks. The hands have now been replaced by digital readouts showing minutes, seconds and hundredths of seconds.

The time displayed on digital clocks is presented as individual units. Traditional dial clocks show time as part of a continuous flow. This difference may subtly affect our perception of time itself.

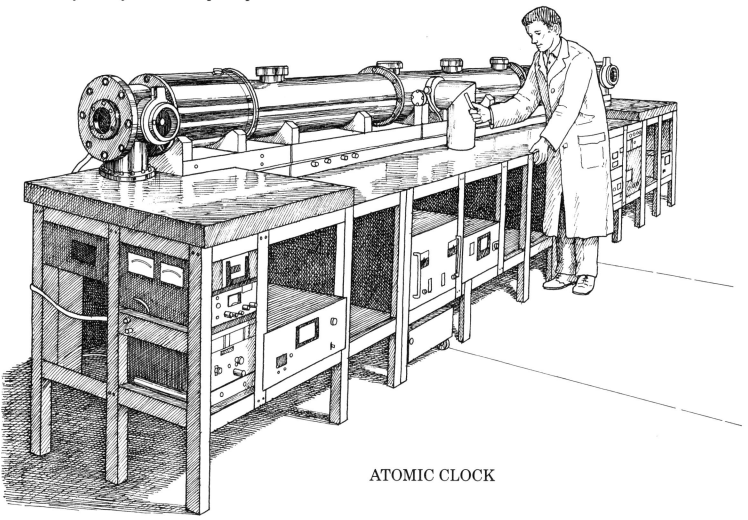

ATOMIC CLOCK

ATOMIC CLOCKS

All of the clocks described so far in this book have depended upon the measuring of a frequency of swing or vibration. This means that they cannot keep going forever. According to the laws of motion observed by Isaac Newton in the 17th century, all objects in motion must eventually run down or lose energy — even the best clocks!

In 1913, a Danish physicist, Niels Bohr, was studying the motion of atoms when he made an important discovery. He realized that the electrons revolving around the nucleus of atoms did not go in a circular motion, losing energy gradually like the planets around the sun. Instead, they jumped between

definite orbits. This process released energy in the form of radiation at a particular frequency.

For years scientists worked on ways of measuring these frequencies. Then, in 1949, the U.S. National Bureau of Standards announced that it had developed the first clock based on the natural frequency of atomic particles. These first atomic clocks used the ammonia molecule as a resonator. This was followed by the cesium resonator. Large cesium-beam tube-resonators maintained in laboratories are accurate to one second every 370,000 years, or a few microseconds each year.

TIME AND SPACE

So far, we have only looked at how time seems to work on our own planet, earth. On earth, all motion, including the function of clocks, appears to be governed by Newton's laws of motion. However, those laws depend on gravity, and when we enter the greater universe of outer space, we begin to realize that Newton's laws do not always apply.

If a spaceship carrying a clock were to travel into deep space and back, the clock's time would be different than the time shown on clocks on earth. The

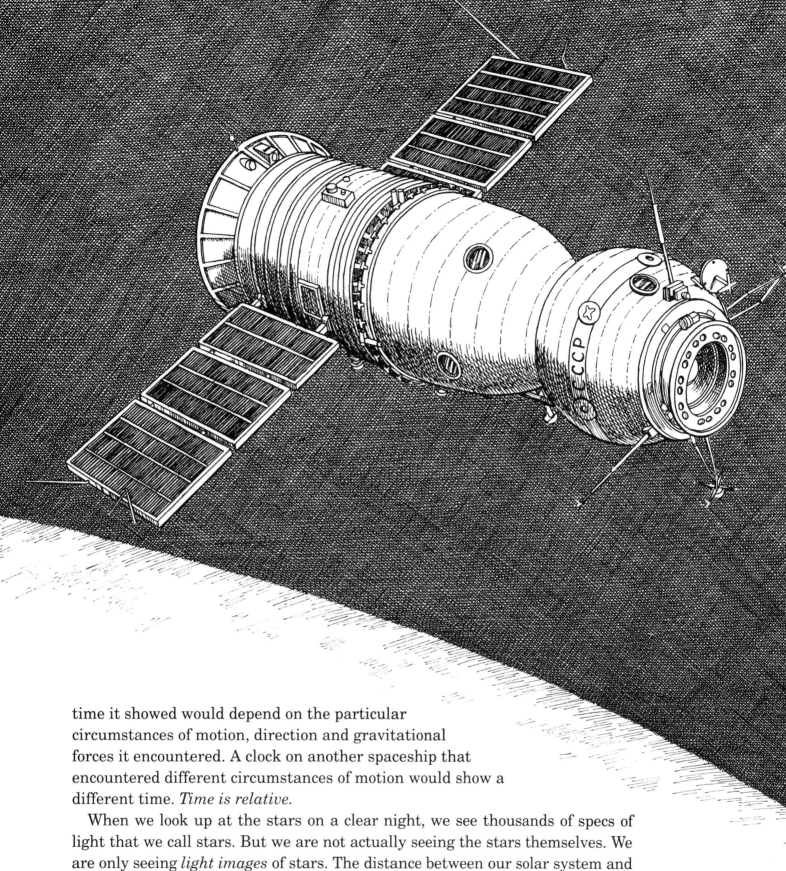

time it showed would depend on the particular circumstances of motion, direction and gravitational forces it encountered. A clock on another spaceship that encountered different circumstances of motion would show a different time. *Time is relative.*

When we look up at the stars on a clear night, we see thousands of specs of light that we call stars. But we are not actually seeing the stars themselves. We are only seeing *light images* of stars. The distance between our solar system and the other stars and galaxies is so great that it is measured in *light-years* — the distance light travels in one year. The speed of light is 186,287 miles (299,792 kilometers) per second. A light-year is about six trillion miles, or ten trillion kilometers! The star nearest to our sun, Proxima Centauri, is 4.3 light-years away. When astronomers observe the explosions of stars (known as *supernovas*), they are actually observing events that occurred thousands of years ago!

In the 20th century, physicists, from Albert Einstein to Stephen Hawking, have explored the nature of time, space and the universe. It is believed by many scientists that we live in an expanding universe that started with a *"big bang."* Recently scientists have discovered regions of space with gravitational forces so strong that even light cannot escape. These are called *black holes.* They believe that if the beginning of time can be measured from the big bang, perhaps the end of time might occur when all matter is drawn into a single black hole — the *"big crunch."*

ASTROLABE. An instrument for measuring the height above the horizon of the sun and stars.

AUTOMATA. Machines that respond automatically. Mechanically controlled.

AUTUMNAL EQUINOX. In the northern hemisphere, the day or time when the sun appears to move south across the equator and day and night are of equal length; about September 22. In the southern hemisphere, this is the vernal equinox.

BOOK OF HOURS. A medieval calendar and prayer book; most often illustrated.

CHRONOLOGICAL. The arrangement of events in the order in which they happen.

CHRONOMETER. A time-keeping instrument. Especially one that keeps very accurate time at all temperatures; used in navigation.

CLEPSYDRA. A water clock; from the words cleps, meaning "thief," and hydra, meaning "water," which describe the escapement of the clock.

EPHEMERIS. A table of calculations showing the positions of the heavenly bodies in the sky on given dates and times; used by early navigators.

ESCAPEMENT. The part of a watch or clock mechanism that holds back and then releases the motive power.

FUSÉE. A cone-shaped device around which a chain connected to the main-spring of a mechanical watch or clock is wound. The taper (slant) of the cone regulated the power of the spring as it wound down.

GNOMON. The rod, pin or angular plate of a sundial. Time is shown by the shadow it casts on the dial.

HOROLOGIST. A person who studies the measurement of time or the making of clocks and watches.

INTERNATIONAL DATE LINE. The line halfway around the world (180°) from the Prime Meridian which runs from the North Pole to the South pole. Travelers who cross the date line from east to west lose a day; those crossing from west to east gain a day.

JACQUEMARTS or JACKS. Mechanical watchmen who struck bells with small hammers to sound the hours on medieval clocks.

LATITUDE. The angular distance of a place north or south of the equator; measured in degrees.

LEAP YEAR. A year with an extra day inserted to ensure that a calendar stays in sequence with the earth's movement around the sun. Once every four years February 29 is added to our calendar to create a leap year.

LONGITUDE. The angular distance east or west of the Greenwich meridian; measured in degrees.

LUNAR CYCLE or LUNATION. The interval between new moons; about 29½ days.

METONIC CYCLE. The 19-year cycle after which extra months and days were added to the Babylonian calendar and its 354-day lunar year. This was done to bring the calendar into conformity with the seasons; named for the Babylonian scholar Meton.

NOCTURNAL. An instrument used to calculate the time at night by marking the progress of the constellations around the North Star.

PRIME MERIDIAN. The longitudinal line from the North to South Pole that passes through Greenwich England.

RUNES. Early alphabetic characters used in northern Europe.

SIDEREAL PERIOD. The time it takes for a planet to make a full journey around the sun as measured against distant stars. The earth's sidereal period, or year, is 365.2564 solar days.

SUMMER SOLSTICE. In the northern hemisphere, the day or time when the sun is farthest north from the equator; about June 21. It is the longest day of the year in the northern hemisphere and the shortest day in the southern hemisphere, where it is the winter solstice.

VERNAL EQUINOX. In the northern hemisphere, the day or time when the sun moves north across the equator and day and night are of equal length; about March 20. In the southern hemisphere, this is the autumnal equinox.

WANING MOON. The moon's apparent decreasing in size as it changes from full to new.

WAXING MOON. The moon's apparent increasing in size as it changes from new to full.

WINTER SOLSTICE. In the northern hemisphere, the day or time when the sun is farthest south from the equator; about December 22. It is the shortest day of the year in the northern hemisphere and the longest in the southern hemisphere, where it is the summer solstice.